LEADERSHIP IN CONFLICT

Leadership in Conflict

The Lessons of History

Steven I. Davis
Managing Director
Davis International Banking Consultants

St. Martin's Press
New York

St. Martin's Press, Scholarly and Reference Division,
175 Fifth Avenue, New York, N.Y. 10010

First published in the United States of America in 1996

Printed in Great Britain

ISBN 0–312–12713–8

Library of Congress Cataloging-in-Publication Data
Davis, Steven I.
Leadership in conflict : the lessons of history / Steven I. Davis.
— 1st ed.
p.   cm.
Includes bibliographical references and index.
ISBN 0–312–12713–8
1. World History.   2. Statesmen—Biography.   3. Leadership.
I. Title.
D21.3.D36   1996
909—dc20   95–22033
                                                      CIP

Contents

Foreword
by James MacGregor Burns

I am one of those Americans who sit transfixed as we watch the question period in the House of Commons on our public television. The direct confrontation of top party leaders, the ranks of supporters arrayed behind them, the blunt and specific questions, the sharp and often snide replies, the presiding officer who is, impressively, a woman, all symbolize for Americans our ideals of parliamentary debate and democracy.

I hope, in this respect, I am not a naive Anglophile. As a teacher of British government for many years in my country, and as a longtime visitor and student in Britain, I know the reservations of the British themselves about their political system – the superficiality of much of the debate, the over-emphasis on 'talking' leadership as against 'doing' leadership, the tedium and triviality of parliamentary proceedings, the popular urges toward third partyism that often seem drained away in an unrepresentative two-party channel. But what in the end most impresses many of us is the success of the parliamentary system in handling both concord and conflict, compromise and competition.

One of the most impressive aspects of the extraordinary work that follows is Steven Davis's concentration on concord and compromise, his concern with the capacity of leadership to deal with conflict. Here he does not fall into the trap of seeking to abolish conflict by calling for consensus, centrism, 'let's all sit down around the table and work things out'. For one thing, he knows that real leaders have strong values and visions that they will not yield to expediency and self-advancement. For another, he is less interested in compromise between parties than in harmony, congruence, agreement between leaders and their own followers.

His skilful discussion of followership brings the author abreast of the current research emphasis in the United States and elsewhere. The idea of leaders as persons barking out orders to followers has long since disappeared. The test of leadership is the extent to which leaders, with values of their own closely related to those of their present and future followers, provide a powerful *collective* leadership that can bring about palpable, measurable and purposeful change.

Emphasizing followership as well as leadership – indeed, seeing these phenomena as inextricably interrelated – immensely complicates the subject. Instead of focusing on the ideas and deeds of a single leader, or group of leaders, one must probe the dynamics of those multitudes that both follow and guide the leadership. Biographies and other accounts of leaders abound, and Steven Davis has well exploited them. Accounts of the multitude, however, are lost, unspoken, unrecorded, or left in dusty attics. The annals of the poor are poor.

Political conflict, economic competition, ideological combat, theological dispute, are the powerhouses of leadership. Skilful but visionary leaders are needed to direct the forces of enmity and ambition into constructive directions. How render conflict, inevitable in any polity but especially in democracies, controllable and creative? How use conflict to strengthen rather than blunt or fragmentize leadership itself? It is one of the great strengths of this work that it seats concord and conflict in a very wide variety of polities, and as carried out by a fascinating diversity of great leaders.

Steven Davis analyses many other aspects of leadership besides conflict – for example, leadership skills, motivation of leaders, and the role of leaders' longevity as well as their impact long after their death or departure from leadership positions. But he wisely eschews a 'laundry list' of leadership traits which may in fact vary widely from leader to leader, country to country and epoch to epoch. Rather he returns over and again to the central role of vision, shared values, a resulting strong sense of direction and the execution of change. But he does not get lost in concepts either. His eclectic and catholic assembly of vivid case-studies of leadership shows the extraordinary variety of ways leaders with strong values and goals go about the enormously difficult – and sometimes dangerous – task of achieving their goals.

This work not only gains from current research as well as from the author's practical leadership experience and from his study of diverse leaders. It also helps set the agenda for future research and writing on leadership. No one is more aware of the limitations of present leadership theory than those working in the field. We need to sort out values in all their variety, vision in all its evocative power, motivation in its many forms, human wants and needs and expectations in all their manifestations, and see how these forces combine and clash in the channels of lasting change. We need to see the varieties of leadership in history, as Steven Davis has given us, but also to discern patterns and similarities that enable us to begin to fashion a comprehensive theory of leadership–followership.

The author calls himself only an amateur student of leadership. If so, he joins the ranks of the rest of us amateurs – there are no experts yet – who are seeking to work out a general theory of leadership that will be tested by its practical application to day-to-day needs and real social progress.

Preface

The gestation period for this book has been a long and complex one. Wandering through the French Alps on a snowy path about 15 years ago, I first began to ponder over the role of the individual leader and how he or she made things happen. What focused my mind was the proliferation of apparently unending conflicts throughout the world – not just in countries like Somalia, Lebanon and Cyprus but also in the 20–30 other regions in which some form of organized violence is recorded by periodic surveys like those of *The Economist*. Could a leader make a difference in bringing people together? Did these unfortunate countries lack leadership, or was the level of conflict simply too powerful for any leader to overcome?

These musings led to a decade of reading in the vast literature on the subject of leadership. I found much scholarship written from a host of perspectives – that of the historian, psychologist, political scientist, sociologist and even student of leadership itself. Theories of leadership abound, yet I found relatively little which seemed to be based on the actual experience of a wide range of acknowledged leaders and how they had addressed schism and conflict. In particular, there was relatively little written on the subject across cultures, past centuries and different fields of human endeavour. Texts on leadership are replete with brief references to selected leaders and the selected case-study. What I found lacking, however, was a more comprehensive survey of such a universe.

Two questions gradually shaped themselves in my mind. First, is there a universal model or paradigm of leadership across cultures, time periods and professions? Secondly, what can the experience of proven leaders throughout history tell us about possible solutions to the seemingly unending current strife between violently opposed religious, ethnic and national groups?

At this point I turned for help to two key individuals. First, Professor James MacGregor Burns, the author of one of the few volumes (Burns, 1978) that both examines actual leadership behaviour and posits a leadership theory based on this behaviour, generously agreed to become my mentor on this project. Without his encouragement and counsel, this book could not have been written. On more than one occasion, having hit a stone wall I turned to Jim Burns, who responded not only with encouragement but also the solution to my problem. Buoyed by this support, I turned to Tim Farmiloe, my editor at Macmillan who had so effectively launched me as an author in my career speciality of banking.

With Tim's support I then commenced several years of selecting and reading the biographies of the leaders who are profiled in this book. In the course of this odyssey, I benefited from the advice and counsel of dozens of authors, historians and friends. On at least one occasion when my will was faltering at the prospect of presuming to make a contribution to such a well-developed literature shaped by so many more qualified authors, I was told – just go do it! I have, and I hope others will enjoy travelling on the same road. Thanks go in particular to Dolores Mulroy, who once again sorted out my incoherent drafts to create a professional final document.

London
October, 1994

Introduction: The Terms of Reference

The conflicts and confrontations which appear to be a permanent feature of the 1990s seem to cry out for a leader who can knit the polarized factions together. The objective of this book is to examine the behaviour of successful leaders to provide insight on how they resolved such conflicts. The innocent observer of this trauma thus finds himself facing the age-old issues: what can a single individual do in the face of such strongly held opposed views? Are these nations bereft of leadership, or have their leaders tried and failed against insuperable odds?

No single volume is likely to resolve these hoary questions, but it should at least be possible to analyse what successful leaders have done throughout history to deal with a high level of conflict. This, then, is a book about such leaders and how they went about their task. It is about the *how*, rather than the *what* or *why* of leadership.

Leadership is a gigantic subject with a literature to match its scope. Simply reading the widely accepted compendium on this literature, Bass and Stogdill's *Handbook of Leadership*, is a Herculean task. In the United States in particular, a well-developed theory and practice of leadership in a business or institutional environment has evolved, led by accomplished authors such as Bernard Bass, Warren Bennis, and James Kouzes. A reasonable consensus exists on the nature of leadership: essentially showing the way and providing direction. John Adair refers to its roots in the ancient Anglo-Saxon *laed*, which refers to a path or road (Adair, 1980: 57).

Yet actually defining leadership requires making a judgement about the morality or value of the leadership. At one extreme, Professor Burns incorporates this value judgement; for him, 'leadership is inducing followers to act for certain goals that represent the values and the motivations – the wants and needs, the aspirations and expectations – of both leaders and followers.' (19). A more common judgement is

1

Rosenbach's 'leadership is all about making things happen that otherwise might not happen ... it is the process of getting people to work together to achieve common goals and aspirations'(xiii). And then there is Harry Truman's flippant 'leadership is the ability to get people to do what they don't want to, and like it' (Bailey: 225). But one cannot evade the issue of morality. As Peter Drucker puts it, 'what really matters is whether the leader leads in the right direction or misleads.'

For the purposes of this book, I have defined leadership quite simply as getting things done through people. As discussed below, I find it necessary to separate the act of leadership from its value or morality, an issue which is addressed in detail in Chapter 5 of Part II. Particularly in an environment of polarized conflict, the leader must achieve results, or make things happen, by virtue of his ability to move or otherwise persuade others to change their behaviour.

On this definition it is clear that leadership is not the province of a favoured few. As Kouzes and Posner point out, 'leadership is not the private reserve of a few charismatic men and women. It is a process ordinary managers use when they are bringing out the best in themselves and others. (1987: xxi). Burns agrees: 'political leadership is ubiquitous and pervasive' (117). Nor is it simply a job title. In the course of our daily lives, all of us play some role in leading our families, friends and colleagues. The issue is one of degree, and this book will focus on the truly exceptional leaders who have moved thousands or millions with repeated and well-documented success.

Another issue raised by this definition is the emotive nature of the term. Motivating people to change their behaviour can be done at one extreme by voluntary consensus: the phrase *a sense of common purpose* is one of the contemporary buzzwords. At the other extreme, however, it can be achieved by purely authoritarian methods deplored by good democrats. This book includes a number of such authoritarians, and Chapter 5 addresses the moral dimension of successful leadership. In a word, can a thoroughly nasty person, intent on building his power-base at the expense of his followers' real interests, be a leader? If so, how can we evaluate the quality of his leadership?

Such a definition also forces the analyst to address the distinction between professional talent or intellectual prowess on the one hand, and on the other the ability to lead people. There is no neat dividing line between the two, but the distinction is an important one. A talented artist like Wolfgang Mozart or a scientist like Albert Einstein can have a powerful impact on others without any leadership skills at all simply by virtue of his professional skills or intellectual power. Yet blending these with true leadership talent extends the individual's reach to enable him or her to lead a group such as a technical laboratory, a football club or a symphony orchestra. As some of the examples of successful military leaders profiled in this book will confirm, one can be a military genius in terms of sensing and capitalizing on tactical and strategic opportunities on the battlefield, yet, without leadership skills in motivating and inspiring his troops, a general is unlikely to make effective use of these purely military talents.

As the ambit of the leadership task increases from a small group to a national electorate or major institutional unit, the relative importance of leadership skills grows correspondingly. As I absorbed the lessons from the biographical material, the relationship between professional/intellectual skills and pure leadership became clearer. At one extreme, leaders with extraordinary professional skills such as Andrew Carnegie in business and Alexander the Great on the battlefield score high on the expertise axis, while others such as Mohandas Gandhi and Abraham Lincoln had little in the way of such prowess but displayed outstanding ability to lead masses of people. Of particular interest to the student of leadership are leaders such as George Washington and Charlemagne who score highly in both dimensions.

Another leadership facet of central importance to this study is scope – the three key dimensions of profession, chronological time and culture. By far the greatest contribution to the literature on the subject of leadership is Anglo-Saxon in origin. More specifically, the American business community has attracted particular interest, and an outpouring of how-to-do-it leadership books graces the shelves of most libraries and book stores. Yet, despite the widely proclaimed globalization of business activity, there is a paucity of research on leadership across national and cultural boundaries. More important, however, from the standpoint of the issue addressed by this book – the universal problem of conflict – is to attempt to de-

termine whether there is a global, universal model or paradigm for successful leadership in conflict.

There is such a paradigm for the American business community, which is well articulated by authors such as Warren
Bennis, Bernard Bass, and James Kouzes. Very briefly, this
model establishes three key dimensions to business leadership:
a challenging vision for the business entity; the ability to
empower or motivate key colleagues to share the vision, and
acting out in daily business life the tenets and values incorporated in the vision.

The task of this book is more ambitious. By selecting a
range of acknowledged leaders from different cultures, time
periods and activities, my objective is to determine whether
this – or any other – paradigm is valid across cultures and dimensions of human effort. Is there, for example, any commonality between the leadership skills of an eighth-century
European emperor, a nineteenth-century English nurse, a
twentieth-century Indian pacifist and a nineteenth-century
American industrialist? Can a seventeenth-century Russian absolute monarch dealing with rebellious subjects be compared
with a nineteenth-century American president confronted
with the outbreak of a civil war? Does a Japanese premier
raised in the Meiji era display the same leadership profile as
his nineteenth-century German counterpart?

Selecting the leaders for this sample was a critical task. At
the outset I determined not to reinvent wheels by undertaking
original research; I therefore relied on published biographical
material, from which I selected one or more texts which provided rich detail on the how, rather than the what or why, of
the leader's achievements. The choice of one among potentially dozens of biographers – especially of personalities like
Napoleon or Tito who evoke strong emotional responses – was
inevitably arbitrary. Suffice it to say that I strove to find a balanced, detailed account which focuses on leadership talent
rather than moral judgement.

I made every effort to achieve some balance across cultures,
activities and time periods. Inevitably, more relevant biographical detail is available on nineteenth- and twentieth-century
subjects, but I deliberately accepted less detail of leadership
approach on earlier leaders to provide such a balance. The
same applies to nationality; with my universe limited to biogra-

phies published in English and French, a similar deliberate effort was made to limit the number of Anglo-Saxon subjects in favour of those representing other cultures. Finally, I tried to balance political leaders with those active in the religious, business, social and public service domains. While acknowledging that a national political leader arguably represents the ideal candidate for the purposes of this book, the inclusion of individuals such as Ignatius Loyola, Albert Schweitzer, Mohandas Gandhi and Florence Nightingale gives some perspective on leaders outside the political mainstream.

The context of conflict was deliberately chosen to delineate and magnify the nature of the leadership task. As Burns points out, leadership and conflict are inextricably linked. 'Leaders do not shun conflict, they confront it, exploit it, ultimately embody it' (39). A similar view is that expressed by that formidable American first lady, Abigail Adams: 'Great necessities call forth great leaders' (quoted in Bennis and Nanus: 91).

Both logic and historical evidence confirm that leadership is truly tested under sharp conflict: civil war, religious conflict, and the presence of polarized political factions. A major subset of leadership literature addresses, for example, the differences between leadership and management. Sound bites like 'doing the right thing (leadership) and doing things right (management)' abound. Yet if one accepts my definition of leadership – getting things done through people – this distinction, like the old one between management and administration, becomes of secondary interest to the basic challenge of convincing people to modify their behaviour. I share John Adair's view that management and leadership overlap to such an extent that the analyst can more usefully address other issues.

Each of the leaders selected has distinguished himself or herself by successfully addressing conflict in its extreme form. Obvious candidates are those who found themselves in the middle of a violent civil war, such as Abraham Lincoln and Henri IV. More common are cases of builders like Kemal Ataturk, Otto von Bismarck, Peter the Great and Isabella of Castile who overcame both internal and external resistance to their vision of a nation state.

The 25 leaders selected are an imperfect sample. I found a relative absence of insightful biographies of Asian, African and

Latin American leaders, which constitutes an obvious cultural gap. On the other hand, arguably the conflicts posed in open, pluralist, democratic states represent a more powerful challenge to leadership than more traditional or autocratic societies. And finding the right geographical balance has meant excluding such remarkable western leaders as Winston Churchill and Franklin Roosevelt. I would have liked to profile more than three outstanding women leaders, but the biographical material was sadly lacking.

Above all, this selection is not intended to be a hall of fame of world leaders. It is rather a best effort at constructing a sample or mosaic which is appropriate for the task at hand – namely to observe a variety of acknowledged outstanding leaders in different cultures, time-frames and professions and how they addressed conflict. A larger sample in my view would be unlikely to generate significantly different findings and conclusions.

In preparing Part I from the biographical source material, I make no claims to be writing superior or even accurate history. I have relied entirely upon the relevant author to present the facts and the leader's actions. This is not the work of a professional historian, but of a seeker of insight into leadership behaviour. For any errors of fact or interpretation by myself or the biographer, I apologize in advance.

Finally, no effort has been made to compare these perceived successful leaders with their less successful counterparts. In selecting the 25 biographies chosen, I encountered many less successful individuals, and parallels will be drawn later in the book between them and the leaders selected. For such a comparative effort, the reader is referred to the recent thoughtful book by Garry Wills, *Certain Trumpets* (1994), which explicitly compares the leadership of 16 pairs of successful and unsuccessful leaders in different professions and roles.

The present book is divided into two sections. Part I provides the summaries of the actual leadership profiles of the 25 individuals, while Part II summarizes my findings and conclusions from the biographies selected. The order could have been reversed, but the format chosen permits the reader to draw his own conclusions from the evidence presented, which can then be compared with my own. The profiles in Part I attempt to extract, in a few paragraphs, the essence of the individual's leadership profile: how did the leader move his followers?

The findings of our analysis commence with Chapter 1 of Part II, which describes how all leaders provide direction, either in the form of values or vision. It gives a brief summary of the direction given by each of the 25 individuals under study. Chapter 2 then evaluates the second common dimension of leadership, the interpersonal skills used to motivate followers. The chapter describes how each leader uses his or her superior insight into human behaviour to obtain tangible results. The final common leadership dimension – the relentless, driven pursuit of the chosen direction in the leader's day-to-day life – is addressed in Chapter 3.

Having thus defined leadership traits, the book then commences its conclusions with Chapter 4, which assesses the actual impact of the chosen leaders on events, both during and after their lifetimes. Chapter 5 then examines the moral dimension of leadership. Having argued that the exercise of leadership itself does not necessarily carry any moral or ethical judgement, we now address this ethical dimension. In effect, how can one distinguish ethically 'good' from 'bad' leadership among individuals who are driven by superior motivation, possess outstanding human insight, and pursue their objective with relentless energy. The concluding Chapter 6 addresses the issue of contemporary leadership. Having eschewed in Part I the analysis of living leaders, the book concludes with some observations on the relevance of the earlier chapters on leadership at the end of the twentieth century.

Part I
Leadership Profiles

The Profiles

The brief profiles of the 25 leaders selected are designed to provide an understanding of how the individual led, as opposed to what he or she achieved or the factors driving the leader's behaviour. The challenge is thus to extract the essence of the leadership dimension from a mass of information not directly relevant to the subject of leadership. Our focus is on the interpersonal relationships of the leader: where he directs his followers, how he motivates them and how in his everyday interactions he sustains the chosen direction.

Each profile attempts to provide just enough insight into leadership behaviour and its historical context to address the issues articulated in the introduction. For the student interested in more detail and understanding of the 'what' or 'why' of the leader, there is no substitute for the underlying biography itself. Liberal use has been made of quotations from these volumes to transmit as much as possible of the biographer's insights and contemporary evidence rather than my own interpretation.

Each profile begins with a brief description of the individual's achievements in the context of the conflicts which he addressed. This effort at establishing the appropriate context is followed by a description of the direction chosen together with the values or vision underpinning that direction.

Subsequent paragraphs describe the techniques used to support the leadership direction: how the leader motivates his followers, what interpersonal techniques are used, how communication takes place, etc. The profile concludes with brief comments on the significance of the leadership period: how it ended, the contribution made by the leader during his or her lifetime, and the role of this contribution in the community's subsequent history. After this summary, there is a case-study of a specific act or process of leadership taken from the biographical material. This case-study provides texture and insight into a particular dimension of the leader's record.

After much thought on the sequence in which the profiles are presented, I decided simply to place them in alphabetical

11

order – rather than chronological, geographical or some other logical ranking. Our objective is not to segment or classify the individual leaders but rather to portray an overall mosaic of behaviour. Thus a simple alphabetical listing should provide the appropriate random selection from which we shall in Part II draw our findings and conclusions.

Alexander of Macedon

The Ultimate Conqueror

Arguably the most successful military commander in recorded history, over a ten-year period beginning in 334BC Alexander of Macedon conquered an empire extending from Greece through the Persian Empire to the Himalayas. He thus achieved his driving personal ambition to become the 'King of all Asia'. Although his leadership skills centred on maintaining the discipline and loyalty of his Macedonian army in pursuit of this personal vision, he also made a determined effort to broaden his base of support to include Persian and other conquered nations.

Alexander was above all a remarkable military commander: resourceful, bold, tenacious and endowed with a unique psychological insight into the minds of both opponents and his own troops. Consistently rejecting the conventional approach or the low-risk solution, he boldly sent home his fleet from Asia Minor and followed the riskier land route, turned his back on revolt in Greece in order to focus on Asia, led his men over the ramparts in besieging Indian cities, and crossed 50 miles of trackless desert by night to achieve an objective. Even when outmanoeuvred – as by Darius at Issus – or outnumbered, he could respond with an ingenious tactical solution.

As a leader, however, Alexander distinguished himself by his insight into human motivation. Retaining the commitment and loyalty of his Macedonian army, however well disciplined and rewarded they were by the spoils of the Persian Empire, was more of a challenge than defeating an enemy army on the battlefield. Thus, having endured countless hardships and risks over eight years on their 17 000 mile march to the Beas

River in Northern India, the army understandably preferred to return to Greece rather than face further unknown dangers in pursuit of Alexander's dream of Asian conquest. He held them together by a combination of bribery, strict discipline and emotional appeals – often followed by his withdrawal to his tent to remind them of their dependence on him to bring them home safely. He thus turned potential disaster into success following his killing of the loyal Cleitus in a drunken brawl by shutting himself up for three days in apparent grief. Only in 326BC at the Beas River did he turn back – and only then after his general Coenus pointed out: 'Sir, if there is one thing above all others a successful man should know, it is when to stop' (Green: 222).

Alexander's leadership challenge was heightened by his commitment to integrate the conquered Persian military and administration into his Greek command structure. While conquest rather than administration was his priority, he recognized the need to win the support of conquered nations as well as fill the gaps in his war machine. Thus Persian formations were integrated into Macedonian battle units, local marriages by his officers encouraged, conquered nations ruled by their own laws and customs, and Persians trained by the thousands to enter his army. While not always successful, this policy of local recognition produced results: thus Porus, the Indian Rajah defeated at the battle of Jhelum, became a loyal governor of his region. While ego as well as wisdom drove his policy of being recognized as the successor to the Persian Achaemenid dynasty, Alexander expended much energy – often to the fury of his Macedonian colleagues – in broadening the base of his support by retaining local structures and tradition. Facing another mutiny over the integration of Persian troops, he won over his Macedonians by saying 'I regard you *all* as my kinsmen' (250).

His persistence and energy in pursuing the goal of conquest extended well beyond the military domain. Seven months – and many casualties – were expended in the siege of the supposedly impregnable city of Tyre; fleets of over 1000 ocean-going craft were built in the Himalayas; three years of bloody guerrilla warfare in the hostile Afghan mountains were spent tracking down the last claimant to the Achaemenid crown; and fierce Himalayan winters were no obstacle to his desire to press on. Had the mutiny at the Beas not occurred, Alexander would undoubtedly have continued south across India.

By his own leadership standards, Alexander's decade of conquest was a successful one. Following his premature death in 323BC, his empire crumbled in a fierce and bloody battle for succession. When asked on his deathbed to name his successor, Alexander responded 'to the strongest ... I foresee a great funeral contest over me' (259) – an indication of his relative lack of interest in ensuring the continuation of what he had created. He had conquered all his enemies, extended his empire to the boundaries of the Persian Empire, held his war machine together, and fully enjoyed the glory he sought. Whether a leader more committed to management rather than conquest could have achieved a more peaceful succession of this massive, complex empire is a moot point. As his biographer Peter Green summarizes his life, 'his true genius was as a field commander: perhaps the most incomparable the world has ever seen. His business was war and conquest ... he spent his life, with legendary success, in the pursuit of personal glory' (260).

Case-Study: Leading from the Front against the Malli

During his decade of conquest Alexander on countless occasions displayed his leadership skills in battle. His conquest of the citadel of the Malli tribe in India on his return down the Jhelum River stands out, however, as a classic example of military leadership from the front.

After eight years of constant campaigning, Alexander's troops were on the verge of mutiny when he stopped his fleet in 326BC to defeat the powerful Malli tribe. His veterans could think only of continuing their return voyage to the safety and luxury of Persia, while Alexander had only further conquest in mind. Having marched his Macedonians over night for 50 miles across a waterless desert, Alexander ordered the scaling ladders erected before the Malli stronghold.

On two occasions his men refused to mount the ladders. Against the advice of a soothsayer, he snatched a ladder himself and mounted it alone with only a light shield for protection. At the top he stood in full view of enemy archers rather than wait for support, then jumped alone into the citadel to face the defenders. Humiliated, his troops finally broke down the postern gate to rescue him, but only after an Indian arrow had lodged deep in his breastbone beside the heart.

After its extraction, Alexander hung a week between life and death, provoking total consternation among his army who saw themselves leaderless deep in enemy territory if he died. In the view of his biographer 'nothing could more clearly demonstrate the personal and charismatic quality of the king's leadership – or its fundamental limitations. All he had built up depended on the awe and inspiration caused by his physical presence' (230). The false rumour of his death produced a revolt in far-off Bactria of Greek mercenaries who set off for home.

But convincing the nervous and suspicious troops that he was alive and recovering was a major task. A public letter to his troops at headquarters was treated as a forgery. Alexander realized that only a personal appearance could stem the breakdown of discipline. Although his wound was still open and he was extremely weak, he ordered his litter to be placed on a platform on his boat in view of the army. Even this was not sufficient to quell the murmuring, so in a remarkable effort of will, he painfully mounted a horse and actually rode into camp, when he was greeted at last by a spontaneous outpouring of relief before he collapsed in his tent.

Arguably he never fully recovered from the effects of his wound and this supreme effort, but he achieved his purpose of restoring morale. The Malli duly surrendered, overwhelmed by the leadership Alexander had shown, and the army resumed its passage down river to the Persian Gulf. The incident also reinforced his hold over the Macedonian army, which once again realized how indispensable he was to their ultimate survival.

The incident truly epitomises Alexander's brand of leadership. A military genius, bold and more self-confident than his followers, he literally led from the front in conquering an entire continent. He drove his men by his personal example, yet, once he had left the scene, his successors were unable to sustain the empire he had personally created.

Kemal Ataturk

Truly the Father of a Nation

From his successful military leadership at Gallipoli in 1915 to his death in 1938, Mustapha Kemal Ataturk played the central role in the creation of the modern Turkey. Rarely has a single individual not only created a new political entity but also infused it with a concept of statehood, a personal vision, and the political foundation which still endures at the end of the twentieth century.

In 1918 Turkey was a defeated member of the Central Powers, the remnant of a disintegrated Ottoman Empire occupied by its Allied conquerors, and a country decades behind its peers in terms of economic wealth and political maturity. Having created from scratch a political and military entity which defeated the occupying Greeks on the battlefield, Kemal successfully negotiated with the Allies the creation of a new nation state and proceeded to transform its culture. The emancipation of women, creation of state industries, abolition of the Caliphate religious state, introduction of the Latin alphabet and the modern Turkish language, and above all a commitment to Western political and economic doctrine – despite the heritage of the war years – were all a personal creation of the new leader.

Military leadership was an essential component of Kemal's success. Trained as a soldier, he was 34 when given the opportunity to demonstrate his leadership skills as a lieutenant colonel defending the Dardanelles against the invading ANZAC army. Until then he had distinguished himself largely as a member of the Young Turk generation committed to the creation of a modern state from the wreckage of the Ottoman Empire. His outspoken views, however, had blocked his political progress in favour of contemporaries such as Enver Pasha.

At Gallipoli, his personal bravery, understanding of the soldier's mentality, strategic instincts and speed of response succeeded in blunting the Allied advance. Leading literally from the front, he personally saved the day for the Turkish defenders in bloody skirmishes which produced a military stalemate on that strategic peninsula.

While his military skills were overshadowed by the subsequent collapse of Turkish resistance on other fronts, they came to the fore again in 1919 when he organized resistance from central Turkey to the Caliphate government, the invading Greeks and other Allies. Communicating with his units by telegraph, he fought off Allied raids on the new capital of Ankara, revolt by dissident Kurds and other tribesmen, and finally confronted the Greek army at the battles of Sakarya and Dumlupinar. In each he commanded personally, often overruling his generals, and combined his military vision with practical skills in timing, anticipation of enemy movements and dissimulation.

A second component of his leadership was a vision of the new Turkey which infused all dimensions of his life. Stirred since his youth in Macedonia, a province of the decaying Ottoman Empire, by the vision of a modern Turkish state able to take its place in a Western-dominated world, he committed himself to a secular, constitutional, and broadly-based state. Turkey's British occupiers thus became his role model of a Western state. As he gathered the reins of power in the 1920s, he personally imposed one reform after another to achieve this vision.

Kemal was also a uniquely skilled communicator and opinion-former, whether with his troops, the Grand National Assembly he had created, the nation as a whole, or a small group of collaborators. In the chaos of occupied Turkey and a disintegrating Caliphate government, he led a small group of reformers committed to his vision. Having convoked in Erzurum the first Grand National Assembly, he spent countless hours with this diverse band in building consensus in the face of opposition from traditional groups and the occupying forces. To direct his scattered and makeshift military forces, he personally manned the telegraph office, which constituted the principal means of communications, for hours on end.

Above all, Kemal was adept at the realistic and pragmatic exercise of power. Persuasion of diverse constituencies in the early days later became a blend of menace, direct speaking and appeals to self-interest as he gathered in the reins of power. Having twice been granted supreme powers in a military emergency by the Assembly for periods of three months, he was denied a third period by a majority vote. Rising from a sick-bed, he won a reversal of the decision by direct appeal. He conceded the formation of a Cabinet but only on condition that he effectively controlled its direction. As his personal power increased, he distanced himself from the four others in his 'band of brothers' who became a liberal opposition and were eventually marginalized. In their stead appeared more pliant colleagues such as Ismet Inonu, his Prime Minister.

Revolts and violence by Kurds and other opponents became the opportunity to eliminate more liberal opposition groups, as Kemal once in power demonstrated an unwillingness to brook opposition.

Kemal's personal leadership style blended an extraordinary willpower, energy and shrewdness with bluntness, lack of polish and a weakness for alcohol. The bottle of raki which often accompanied the hours of late-night communication, eventually led to the cirrhosis of the liver to which he succumbed at the age of 57. This man of action was constantly in motion, questioning those near him and focusing on the issue at hand.

Of particular interest to the student of leadership is Kemal's exercise of power in contrast to that of contemporaries such as Hitler and Stalin. Having gained undisputed power in the 1920s, Kemal was clearly in a position to exercise it to the detriment of the national interest. Purges of the opposition in the late 1920s – including some of his original team – are reminiscent of Stalin's later efforts. Yet Kemal's leadership was driven by his vision of the best interests of Turkey and guided by the role model of Britain. He specifically criticized Napoleon and his Macedonian compatriot Alexander for neglecting their country's interests in favour of personal ambition.

Case-Study: Building a Legislature in 1920
When the Allied occupying forces took over the Turkish parliament in Istanbul in 1920, Kemal (he did not assume the surname Ataturk until 1935) brought together in Ankara a Grand National Assembly which was to become the legislative embodiment of the new nationalist republic. How he organized and led this body is a case-study in his use of internal discussion, threats and appeal to a national vision to achieve his potentially contradictory goals of a representative Western-type democracy and effective personal control over the political process.

The conflict between these goals was apparent at the outset. The delegates comprised a wide universe of social and political backgrounds: Kemalist loyalists, members of the Istanbul-based predecessor body and local leaders with no experience of democratic institutions. Many were deeply suspicious of Kemal's motives.

To bring these disparate elements together, Ataturk employed two strategies: intense discussion, and the election of the entire executive by the assembly, a tactic used to convince the assembly that it was controlling the democratic process. Ataturk then engaged in an intense lobbying compaign of individual legislators through nightly visitations to them in their quarters at the Teachers Training School. With some reluctance, President Arif of the old legislative was persuaded to step down to Vice President of the new one in favour of Kemal as President. To delegates with little or no political experience, he lectured on the meaning of democracy with its sovereignty of the people. After a short debate, the Assembly accepted his proposal and elected Kemal and his team as President and Cabinet. A constituent committee then spent nine months debating a new constitution, with Kemal pushing through a structure based on popular sovereignty but ignoring the role of the existing Caliphate and monarchy.

In the critical months that followed, Kemal was preoccupied with defending the existence of the Nationalist government against attacks by the Greek army and other Western powers, as well as rebellions by local Turkish rival leaders. The Assembly, comprised primarily of such Anatolian notables and clerics, watched critically as the Republic struggled for survival. Daily Kemal would attend the Assembly's meetings to explain and defend his policy, restore order when emotion ruled, and focus their attention on long-term objectives. In the words of Lord Kinross, confronted with the din of hecklers and opposing rhetoric, 'in that clear resounding voice which combined the accents of persuasion and authority, he would continue to expand his arguments, his ideas, his demands. The charm would begin to work, their voices to acclaim him, their hands to rise in an affirmative vote' (269). From time to time, the mask fell in discussion with his closest collaborators. To Halide Edib he burst out saying, 'I don't want any consideration, criticism, or advice. I will have only my own way. All shall do as I command' (272).

But his persuasion paid off. When a powerful local Katahyan warlord and deputy in the Assembly, Ethem, threatened to use his troops to take over the Nationalist Army, the Assembly supported Kemal in open debate and agreed to send a expedition to incorporate Ethem's force in the army. After the defeat by the Greeks at Eskishehir, Ataturk built on the Assembly's consternation and fear of disaster to obtain for himself the delegation of full powers for three months as commander-in-chief.

As the Nationalist government took shape and the military tide turned in its favour, a growing divergence occurred between Kemal's autocratic convictions and those of close collaborators like Rauf who believed in a working democracy with a formal opposition party in the Assembly. Ataturk formed his own party, the Defence of Rights group, to support him in the Assembly. The opposition persuaded him to give up direct control of the Cabinet, which would be headed by Rauf. When the date for the next renewal of extraordinary powers came, three of Ataturk's closest colleagues – Rauf, Refet and Ali Fuad – spent an entire night with him to persuade Ataturk to relinquish these powers. In his speech the next day Ataturk promised to step down to become a private citizen again, but only after military victory had been won. The Assembly proceeded to extend his powers as commander-in-chief, without time limit, until such final victory occurred.

In a similar vein, Ataturk's blend of persuasion and menace won the debate over the sensitive issue of the abolition of the Sultanate, with its temporal power, and the restriction of the power of the Caliphate to a religious role. After his reference to heads rolling if the Assembly did not agree, an Assembly committee approved Ataturk's draft proposal which was subsequently voted by acclamation in the full Assembly.

The first Grand National Assembly met for the last time in April 1923, in the wake of a violent debate over the unsuccessful peace negotiations in Lausanne. Kemal was determined to elect a new, more responsive parliament, and in the decades to come the battle between President and Opposition would continue. Yet he had indeed created a democratic institution in 1920 which, shaped by his persuasion and threats has survived a host of subsequent challenges.

Bismarck

Realpolitik in the National Interest

Exercising his leadership through his patron Kaiser William, Otto von Bismarck during his 28 years in power shaped modern Germany from a collection of independent states into the most influential land power in late nineteenth century Europe. All his energies were focused on the goal of building such a dominant state which effectively provided him with an outlet for his own personal drive for influence and power. In what has become a classic example of *realpolitik*, Bismarck reversed alliances, switched party loyalties, manipulated allies and opponents – all with this supreme objective in mind.

To achieve this single goal, Bismarck blended an overpowering will, a deep understanding of individual behaviour, and a willingness to use any means – including deceit, flattery, bullying and threats – to advance the cause of a united and powerful Germany. Without a natural power-base, he gained and held his unique position by dominating the relatively weak-willed Kaiser through, in turn, his ability to control the Prussian legislature, appealing to the Kaiser's personal preferences, and in general becoming the indispensable Prime Minister. His biographer Edward Crankshaw terms Bismarck a manipulator, not a leader, but he was incredibly effective in the sense of motivating and mobilizing both his nominal superior and a host of domestic and foreign constituencies. In the words of this biographer, 'he was the cleverest man in Europe and the most skilled in statesmanship; his vision ... was almost blindingly intense' (Crankshaw 1981: 305).

While the less liberal dimensions of his leadership style have naturally attracted criticism, the student of leadership is drawn to Bismarck's deep insight into the motives and especially weaknesses of others and the range of weapons he could deploy to exploit this insight. From his first appointment in 1862 as Minister President to William, he demonstrated according to his biographer 'that inborn ability to decide when it was necessary to push hard, when not, which was to be his trademark' (42).

The range of his persuasive armoury was vast: 'a combination of personal magnetism, charm, menace, rudeness, arrogance, irony, delicacy, brutality, humour, deceitfulness, openness, gentle candour and deep-dyed cynicism' (140). All of these interpersonal talents were required at one time or another as Bismarck lured neighbouring states into the wars he used to build Prussia's power-base, enticed independent princes to join the new German Confederation, or bullied the Prussian legislature into supporting his policies.

This remarkable armoury was deployed with a single goal: the creation of the most powerful state in Europe. Friendships, traditional foreign alliances and political relationships were discarded or reversed as Bismarck set the stage for wars of conquest with Denmark, Austria and France which led to the formation in 1870 of the new German state under Prussian leadership. His drive for personal power was thus channelled, through his personal dominance over the Kaiser, into an all-encompassing commitment to building the new state.

Bismarck's towering energy and strength of purpose were fully employed in the exhausting tasks of controlling and guiding the Kaiser, parliament, the army and the other European powers. His 'galvanic, convulsive vitality [was] harnessed to a single end' (15). The pressure on him was intense, and periodically he would collapse physically and retire to his country estate for months at a time.

Within two years of the death of the Kaiser, Bismarck was dismissed by the new Kaiser William II and left the political scene. His personal achievement in building the German state remained intact, although Bismarck has been criticized for creating a state in which the unchecked growth of militarism following his departure in 1890 ultimately led to World War II. One of the fascinating unknowns of history is whether Bismarck would have been able to avoid war had he remained in effective control of the German state.

Case Study: Establishing Dominance over King and Parliament

Central to Bismarck's leadership was his relationship with King William, which in turn was based on his ability to dominate the elected Prussian *Landtag*. In this complex interaction Bismarck could use his repertoire of persuasive talents to appeal to the needs – and weaknesses – of each constituency.

William selected Bismarck in 1862 as Minister President solely because of his perceived ability to dominate the Prussian legislature – in particular to ensure that sufficient financial and other support was provided for the Prussian army he prized so highly. With no ministerial experience or political party behind him, Bismarck would have to rely entirely on his personal leadership skills to meet this challenge.

The battle was quickly joined. In an early policy speech to parliament, he referred to 'iron and blood' which would decide the great issues of the day rather the debates of the 1848 revolution. A storm of liberal protest reached King William, who returned to Berlin to reprimand – and possibly dismiss – Bismarck as his principal minister. Bismarck decided to intercept him at a railway station south of Berlin and justify his position before the King could reach Berlin and be won over by Bismarck's enemies. There ensued an extended interview on the royal train in which Bismarck successfully appealed to William's sense of heroic destiny as the head of the Prussian state fighting for glory and Prussian values.

Another challenge to his relationship with William took place the following year, when Bismarck persuaded William in August 1863 to scuttle an alliance of the German princes designed to revitalize the German Confederation in Frankfurt under Austrian leadership. Not only Franz Joseph of Austria but also Prince John of Saxony, a respected friend of William's, appealed to the Prussian monarch on behalf of his fellow rulers to join them in Frankfurt. Bismarck rose to the challenge to Prussia's leadership by appealing to William's sense of Prussia's primacy – in particular his prized army which might be degraded by being combined with lesser units from the rest of Germany. '. . . the King, worried to the point of exhaustion, torn between his dynastic instincts, his appreciation of the unparalleled gifts of his new chancellor, and his profound distaste for Bismarck's methods, lay on a sofa' (Crankshaw 198: 160). With William reduced to tears after Bismarck's concentrated assault, Bismarck used threats to beat other monarchs like King John into line. The outcome was the failure of the Congress of Princes, which had no meaning without Prussia's participation.

The other side of the leadership coin for Bismarck was the *Landtag*; he could only retain his power over William if he produced satisfactory results from this elected parliamentary body. Under the Prussian constitution, Bismarck as Minister President was responsible to the King, not Parliament. In 1862, the liberals dominated parliament with an overwhelming majority. Yet they were divided internally as well as threatened by the hereditary conservatives on the right and the growing proletariat on the left. But their most important enemy of all was the army, which in turn was William's pride and joy. Bismarck attacked them across the board: by supporting the King on resources for the army, by threatening to go over their heads by using the popular vote in favour of the sovereign, and by appealing to their patriotism through the victories in the three wars he engineered. His principal weapon, however, in retaining William's vital support was support for the plan of three years' military service. He thus prorogued parliament in October 1862, ignored an amendment to the budget, and attacked its successor for assaulting the integrity of the monarchy. In 1863 Bismarck introduced the Press Decree to ban newspapers whose articles might be interpreted to jeopardize the public welfare. The King resisted on the grounds that the sanction offended the spirit of the constitution, but once again Bismarck persuaded him to sign the decree.

In the wake of the victory over Austria in 1866, Bismarck leveraged his popularity to create his own political party, the National Liberals. At the same time he acknowledged, through a bill of indemnity, that he had behaved unconstitutionally during the past four years but requested retrospective approval for unauthorised expenditures. Grouping businessmen, liberals and others for whom Prussian nationalism was a key objective, the new party enabled Bismarck to rule through Parliament for years to come.

In sum, Parliament had no effective response to a prime minister who retained the confidence of the King, in particular one like Bismarck who was determined to pursue his goal of Prussian political and military supremacy. Thus when the liberal Karl von Twesten attacked the army bill during the war with Denmark and threatened to refuse to support the government, Bismarck could simply turn his back and walk out of the chamber. Bismarck's success in manipulating the other German princes as well as foreign powers was legendary, yet without his ability to dominate Parliament and therefore William, he would have had no power-base at all.

Simon Bolivar

A Warrior's Vision of Conquest

In the two decades after he personally declared war in 1809 on the Spanish rulers of Latin America, Simon Bolivar emerged as the Liberator and effective dictator not only of his native

Venezuela but also of present-day Colombia, Ecuador, Peru and Bolivia. He thus successfully emulated his personal hero Napoleon Bonaparte in building a continental empire which had, either by persuasion or military force, granted him total political power. To achieve this goal he had to defeat not only superior armies from the Spanish homeland but also a host of other local dictators and generals as well as deal with the general apathy of most of the local population and the latent class conflicts between the white Creole aristocracy, Indians and mixed-race citizens.

What distinguished Bolivar from his rivals for power as the Spanish American empire slowly disintegrated was the vision he articulated of a continent-wide struggle for independence against the Spanish monarchy. As a wealthy young Creole born in Latin American of Spanish stock and travelling in Napoleonic Europe in the early 1800s, Bolivar vowed at the age of 22 in Rome to emulate Napoleon by overthrowing monarchies in favour of republican regimes committed to representative democracy. Whereas other local revolutionaries sought only personal power, Bolivar cloaked his ambition in republican dress and extended it throughout the Spanish-speaking Latin American continent. Salvador de Madariaga held that: 'it was the ambition to emulate the splendours of an imperial life, to be sun of a solar system of resplendent marshals and the star that draws to itself the ovations of a whole continent that made Bolivar a knight errant in the service of the freedom of South America' (de Madariaga: 68).

To achieve this vision, Bolivar's leadership centred on his overwhelming will to power – essential personal power. Recovering from countless military defeats and other setbacks, Bolivar could rely on 'his will power, that diabolic tension of a Promethean will which is the root cause of his greatness' (167). While his rivals for power may have been better generals or diplomats, de Madariaga notes that 'the only leading, inspiring mind and will was Bolivar's ... he differed from the others in that his vision was truly national, indeed continental, in scope. Hence his constancy, his faith, his will ever taut in the struggle' (321). When he and his rival for continental power, San Martin, finally met after Bolivar had effectively secured power in Ecuador, San Martin acknowledged Bolivar's superior will by admitting that 'the Liberator has stolen a march on us'. (440)

Yet his will to power was limited to military dominance and the glory accruing to the battlefield victor. On attaining power, Bolivar would invariably name a Vice-President to run the country while he left for the next battlefield or conquest. As he himself acknowledged, 'war is my element; danger my glory' (547). Administration – especially the challenges of re-building the war-torn economies through which his armies marched – had no appeal to him: 'I do not want little govern-ments; I am resolved to die under the ruins of Colombia fighting for its fundamental law and for absolute unity' (449). The net result was a sharp deterioration in economic condi-tions as the sophisticated Spanish administration was replaced by a host of short-term measures designed largely to finance and man Bolivar's military machine.

His indomitable will was reflected in a remarkable resilience and persistence. Although a competent general who moved decisively and speedily to attack the enemy, Bolivar suffered his share of serious military defeats in the 1810–20 period. On three separate occasions he was forced to flee Venezuela for a Caribbean exile before returning with yet another invasion force he created from scratch. Unable to win total power in Venezuela against other regional dictators such as Jose Antonio Paez, in 1819 he decided to shift his efforts to win control of an equally divided New Granada (present-day Colombia). He was equally prepared to attack an opposing force or to reach a compromise with its leader: what was im-portant was Bolivar's superior authority. His resistance and de-termination failed only in 1830 when, weakened by illness and tortured by doubts over the validity of his vision, he declined to accept the offer of renewed authority in Colombia and de-parted for voluntary exile.

Paired with this resilience was a ruthlessness in eliminating any opposition to his exercise of power. Bolivar was an early advocate of the 'fight to the death' policy of the Venezuelan insurgents which condemned in advance to death, often as captured prisoners, any Spaniard offering armed resistance. To obtain a passport and the freedom to escape Venezuela after his defeat in 1812, Bolivar turned over to the Spanish au-thorities Francisco Miranda, his superior in the revolutionary struggle. Terror was a weapon in Bolivar's armoury which was wielded with little personal concern for its victims, whether a rebellious city such as Pasto in Colombia or his rival Piar in Venezuela. Writing about his efforts to extract resources for Ecuador, Bolivar notes that 'I know better than anyone how far violence can go, and all has been used' (456).

But Bolivar was also skilled in adapting the message to the audience – in effect telling various constituencies what they wanted to hear. His own and enemy generals as well as constituent congresses were subjected to well-crafted flattery. As he himself wrote about his plans to subvert an armistice signed in 1820, 'I went to that interview armed from head to foot, with my policy and my diplomacy well concealed under an ample show of frankness, good faith and friendship' (384). One of Bolivar's classic techniques was to suggest a course of action which was bound to cause a reaction in favour of his desired goal. Thus electoral congresses in Angostura (1818) and Cucuta (1821) responded to Bolivar's threat to resign with an offer of unlimited executive power – a tactic which was repeated until 1830 when Bolivar for the first time declined such an offer and retired from political life. While the adulation he received as a conqueror entering a capital city may reflect the residents' fear as much as the capture of hearts and minds, Bolivar was adept at reaching out to mass audiences with a magnetic charm, well-turned phrases and a quick wit. 'As a leader he showed the utmost skill and imagination in setting up before the crowd scenes, myths and legends of a dramatic force such as the crowd needs to remain faithful to a cause' (227).

Over time, however, the hypocrisy of his messages became, in the words of de Madariaga, 'a tissue of sophisms, a farrago of empty slogans'; he was an 'unscrupulous pamphleteer'. For Bolivar, words were simply a means to an end, and outright lies as well as misleading interpretations were justified if they supported the extension of his personal power. And the variety of audiences was vast; Bolivar cited 'this outstanding chaos of patriots, Goths (Spaniards), egoists, whites, coloured men, Venezuelans, Cundinamarcans, republicans, aristocrats, good and bad people' (412). When words failed, however, force achieved Bolivar's objective. Thus the independent region of Guayaquil in Ecuador was compelled to join the Colombian empire by the judicious use of bribery, flattery and military force, while in 1828 Bolivar at the Ocaña constitu-

tional convention was obliged to declare himself *Libertador* of
Colombia when he was unable to gain a majority by democratic vote.

His leadership came to an end in 1830 when a combination
of ill health and discouragement caused Bolivar to ignore yet
another call from his partisans in Bogota to assume power.
Internal doubts about the validity of his vision had multiplied
over the years. Not only had role models like Napoleon and
peers like Iturbide in Mexico and San Martin in Chile failed
or retired from their revolutionary mission, but also Bolivar
probably recognized that he was simply replacing an autocratic Spanish monarchy with an equally dictatorial national
regime imposed on citizens who in large part preferred the
Spanish alternative. The success of his rival Paez in declaring
Venezuela independent of Colombia was replicated by similar
moves by Peru and Bolivia out of the Bolivarian orbit.

Judged by the criterion of his subject's welfare, Bolivar's
achievements were mixed. Decades of bloody civil war and
revolt against Spain produced heavy taxes, the massacre of
civilians and soldiers, and the destruction of three centuries of
Spanish civilization – without a compensatory rebuilding of
national economic and social structures. The myth propa-
gated by Bolivar of national independence has remained a
significant element of Latin America history, yet even Bolivar
must have realised that by 1830 his battle cry of replacing
Spanish despotism with American freedom was a hollow one.
In the view of his biographer, 'he was endeavouring to plaster
together, with republican and federative cement, the old
Spanish building he had all but demolished with his political
explosive' (491).

Case-Study: Scaling the Andes to Conquer New Granada

After a decade of revolutionary efforts in his native Venezuela,
Bolivar found himself blocked not just by Spanish forces but
also the resistance of independent generals such as Paez who
refused to subordinate themselves to his leadership. At the
same time, Bolivar was increasingly aware of the threat to his
continental leadership from the Argentine José de San Martin
who was moving north to liberate Chile and eventually Peru.

In a bold stroke which involved risking his leadership in un-
charted waters, Bolivar in 1819 resolved to transport his

Venezuela army westward over the Andes to New Granada to intervene in the struggle there against the Spanish overlords. The odds against him challenged Bolivar's passion for military glory. His army of roughly 3000 men was composed largely of ill-equipped recruits from the plains of Venezuela who were known for desertion in the face of danger, whereas Spanish forces in New Granada numbered some 10 000 well trained and supplied soldiers. Having deliberately picked the most difficult pass – Pisba Moor – to cross so as to surprise the enemy, Bolivar had to traverse 100 miles of rivers swollen by the rainy season to reach the pass.

For such a challenge, Bolivar was at his leadership best. He was 'capable of an untiring physical and moral activity, ... never complained ... for whom no hardship was unbearable, no march too long, no task too menial; who would cheerfully load mules and canoes, or swim his horse back and forth to help across the river weak soldiers or women' (343).

Once the army had crossed into New Granada, he unleashed an eloquent but untruthful appeal for the local population to rally to his victorious liberating army. In four days he energetically prepared his exhausted army for battle and engaged the Spanish general Barreiro. Whereas a prudent general would have avoided battle, Bolivar impatiently attacked and fought an inconclusive eight-hour battle on the Gameza River and another at Vargas. In the latter battle, the day was saved for Bolivar by an attack from his British mercenaries who formed a reliable backbone to his small army. He proclaimed martial law under which all men between 14 and 40 were to present themselves for military duty under pain of being shot, thereby boosting his army from the 1800 men to which it had been reduced by desertion, exhaustion and battle. A bold night march gained him entry to the regional capital of Tunja, and the next day a full-scale battle was fought at the bridge of Boyaca. Bolivar's forces defeated Barreiros, who surrendered with 1600 men. On discovering that one of these men, Vivoni, had betrayed him seven years previously, Bolivar had him executed on the spot. Several days later Bolivar entered the capital, Bogotá, unopposed after the Viceroy Samano had fled.

In retrospect, Bolivar's political sense had matched his military prowess. New Granada was in an unstable political state due to the brutal policy of the Viceroy, and the bold gesture of occupying the capital swung the balance of opinion in his favour. The prisoners he took were largely Venezuelans who rallied to his cause and enabled Bolivar to mop up the remaining Spanish forces in New Granada. Taking over the government, Bolivar assumed full powers, delegated civil authority to his loyal general Santander, and proceeded to confiscate Granadian wealth to feed and arm his troops.

This lightning descent into New Granada thus reflects all of Bolivar's leadership qualities. An unquenchable will to succeed, combined with a resourceful and resilient strategy to swing the odds in his favour, is implemented with a ruthlessness which accepts no compromise.

Napoleon Bonaparte

A Choice between Glory and the National Interest

In a 15-year period between grasping power on 18 Brumaire in 1799 and his exile to Elba, Napoleon Bonaparte transformed France in terms of military power, economic strength, criminal and civil law, the role of the Catholic religion and educational systems. His leadership before the turning-point in 1808 is a classic example of a successful general whose leadership skills extended to the political domain, while his subsequent failure reflected a shift in values from those embodied in the French revolution to the pursuit of national glory for its own sake. In both his rise and his fall, however, Napoleon's leadership was driven by an overpowering will which sought to project and export values to which he was totally committed.

From the initiation of his career as a young lieutenant in revolutionary France, Napoleon was personally committed to the revolution's values of personal freedom, justice and equality. Although a member of the minor nobility and deeply concerned about the revolution's excesses, he blended moderate, family values with this commitment and shot to prominence in successfully defending the Directorate against the Paris mob in 1794. As the remarkably successful commander of the French army in Italy in 1797, he exported these values to conquests which eventually included Northern Italy, Egypt, Switzerland, Belgium, Western Germany, the Netherlands and Poland. A typical Napoleonic programme would include extension of the suffrage, the introduction of representative institutions, restoration of public finances, a major public works programme, and the elimination of traditional privileges.

As the Empire incorporating these values extended to roughly half of Europe, with a population of 70 million, Napoleon added glory and honour to these revolutionary values. In his coronation oath as Emperor in 1804 – reflecting the example of Charlemagne a millennium earlier – Napoleon swore 'to rule for the interests, happiness and glory of the people of France' (Cronin: 253). Although he henceforth bore the title of Emperor and brooked little opposition to his role, Napoleon insisted that he was still a republican and committed to the values of the 1789 revolution.

His leadership success – and ultimate failure – was rooted in his ability as commanding general to win battles. From his first engagement as a revolutionary artillery commander at the 1793 siege of Toulon, Napoleon combined the classical military talents of speed of response, boldness, decisiveness and originality of response to win a string of battles, until finally checked in Russia in 1812. In leadership terms, his military genius included the ability to enforce rigorous discipline at the same time as motivating his troops to superlative levels of performance. Beginning with the award of ceremonial swords and flags to French soldiers distinguishing themselves on the northern Italian battlefield and culminating in the introduction of the Légion d'honneur, Napoleon was a master in generating outstanding military performance by the use of 'baubles ... [with which] men are led. You imagine that an enemy army is defeated by analysis? Never!' (205).

Napoleon's military skills were used to reinforce and drive a set of personal values which meshed to a considerable extent with that of his French constituency. Although post-revolutionary France continued to be riven by political and religious conflict, the great majority of Frenchmen espoused the revolutionary values of equality, justice and personal freedom to which Napoleon was committed. While many Frenchmen re-

joiced in the military glories associated with his victories, the
export of revolutionary values also generated widespread
support among newly enfranchised classes abroad. When political stability and economic growth were also produced by
Napolonic measures, a virtuous circle was created. Although
prepared to apply censorship or close down a democratic institution such as the Tribunate, Napoleon fully believed in his
democratic commitment at home and abroad. 'It is I who
embody the French revolution' (243). Abroad, his instructions
to his sister Pauline on taking administrative responsibility in
Rome in 1803 included 'conform to the customs of the
country; never run down anything, find everything splendid,
and don't say "we do this better in Paris"' (269).

Associated with his revolutionary values of equality and
justice was a commitment to listen – and a corresponding
insight into the thoughts of his followership. Opposition jour-
nalists, clerics and legislators were encouraged to engage in a
one-on-one dialogue. Napoleon plunged deeply into debate
with the Consulate's other institutions on elements in the Civil
Code, the religious settlement incorporated in the 1802
Concordat, and the reform of French education. When confronted with an opposing majority among his advisers, as in
the battle for Russia in 1812 or in elements of the Civil Code,
he was usually prepared to concede the point. His statement
that 'my policy is to govern men as the majority wish' (212)
was confirmed particularly in the savage religious debate
between constitutional and non-juror factions following his assumption of power described in the case-study below.

Yet the dominant element of Napoleon's leadership profile
was his strong will. As a leading biographer comments, 'if
Napoleon's principles can be summed up in the word moderation, the will behind them was wholly immoderate. His will
drew its extraordinary strength from two elements ... love of
honour and love of the French republic ... together they
made the most unyielding will known in history' (191). The
converse of Napoleon's extraordinary will-power and inner
discipline was a ferocious impatience and bluntness – even to
his friends – when crossed. Thus, having returned on his own
authority from command in Egypt in 1799, he impatiently
elbowed his way into political power on 18 Brumaire when
unable to convince the majority of the Directorate to bring

him legally into the political process. Having installed himself as First Consul in the Tuileries Palace, as he himself put it, 'the ox has been harnessed: now it must plow' (194). And plough he did: for the next 15 years he personally initiated – and rigorously followed up – thousands of measures which transformed the economic, political, religious and military dimensions of France and its growing Empire. His biographer notes the 'pulsating activity' associated with Napoleon. Unlike other successful conquerors, Napoleon was a extraordinary administrator as well; as he puts it, 'I am exceptional in [that] I am fitted for both an active (military) and a sedentary (administrative) life' (259). Whether as a soldier or administrator, Napoleon focused his disciplined energy on one issue after another. Enforcing discipline was a central element of Napoleon's leadership. He continually criticized his brother Louis's leadership in Holland, writing: 'When a King is said to be a good fellow, his reign is a failure. How can a good fellow … bear the burdens of royalty and keep malcontents in order?' (264).

His greatest weakness was the impatience which accompanied the exercise of his will: an investigator for the Directorate reporting on Napoleon's performance in Italy noted that 'he has only one guide – the Constitution. But General Bonaparte is not without defects. He does not spare his men sufficiently. Often he demands things in too hasty a manner' (123). Arguably his greatest military failure, the decision to retreat from Moscow in 1812 rather than winter there, could be attributed to Napoleon's impatience. His biographer Vincent Cronin notes that 'impatience was so woven into the fabric of his character that he failed to notice it' (330).

The sum total of these leadership strengths and weaknesses was a 15-year roller-coaster ride from obscurity to a Charlemagne-like prominence and back to total defeat – in military terms as well as for republican virtues at the hands of royalist repression. Hubris – in the form of the pursuit of national glory rather than the true interests of France and its republican values – played a central role in Napoleon's failure. While Napoleon vigorously denied any interests in personal power ("I acted not [on 18th Brumaire] from love of power but because I felt I was better educated, more perceptive and better qualified than anyone else" [167]), his remarkable military success drove him eventually to focus on a glory which benefited himself as much, if not more, than France. As the balance of power in Europe swung away from him, Napoleon repeatedly made choices – the attack on Russia, intervention in Spain, refusal to surrender Belgium – which were driven by his sense of honour rather than that of France's real interests. 'He failed to see that the mass of people, whether Parisians or the men and women of the Empire, or soldiers like Marmont, were unequal in the long run to the heroic role for which he had cast them. Napoleon did not really understand human nature' (366). When military success ultimately eluded him, his leadership collapsed.

Yet Napoleon's values, will and energy have made a permanent imprint on France. In a few years he personally led the efforts to reform French education, introduce the Code Napoleon, create a new financial structure and craft a religious Concordat – most of which have endured for almost two centuries. Although not all Frenchmen – much less foreigners who were ruled by French governors before 1814 – share Napoleon's view of national glory, an independent visitor cannot help but remark on the pride of most Frenchmen today in his achievements.

Case-Study: Shaping the 1802 Concordat

One of Napoleon's most significant and lasting leadership achievements was the religious reconciliation in the form of the 1802 Concordat signed with Pope Pius VII. Crafting this compromise required a deep understanding of the sentiments of his countrymen as well as his negotiating partners – plus a massive dose of his well-known forcefulness, will and deeply felt personal values.

One of the unresolved issues inherited by Napoleon in 1799 was the polarized religious conflict between the constitutional clergy (which accepted the Revolution and the effective disestablishment of the Catholic Church in France) and the nonjuror priests (who refused to do so and accepted only the Pope's authority). The result was bloody civil war which lasted over seven years in the Vendée region in the West of France and ensured the effective closure of French churches to worshippers. Although not deeply religious himself, Napoleon was well aware of the average Frenchman's desire to return to some form of normalized worship – 'to give us back our Sunday'.

Finding a solution however, required delicate negotiations with both the Pope and his own constitutional authorities. To lead the papal negotiations, Napoleon skilfully selected Etienne Bernier, a former Catholic guerrilla leader from the Vendée. Napoleon insisted on two negotiating objectives: a total replacement of existing bishops to enable him to inject new blood into the episcopate, and the retention of all church property which had been nationalized. Arguments raged over whether Roman Catholicism would be an official religion or simply that of the majority of the French people. Nine drafts later – interspersed with regular Napoleonic threats to break off negotiations – the right language was found and the Concordat signed by Napoleon and the Pope. Napoleon had won his main points, and Catholicism was not to be the state religion but that of 'the great majority of the French people'. Yet the battle was far from over. Gallican resistance in Napoleon's Council of State held ratification up for almost a year. The end result was a total of 70 'organic articles' – effectively riders to the basic Concordat – which were added and enabled Napoleon to obtain the Tribunate's approval, but only by seven votes.

Implementing the new Concordat, which Cronin describes as the most popular single act of Napoleon's rule, was equally important. For Napoleon with his deep sense of practicality and family values, 'useful' prelates and monks acting as conciliators had to replace political appointees. The 60 bishops he chose included 32 who had never before held a see. Franciscans and Dominicans, but not Trappists, who were excluded as 'not useful'. Thus according to Napoleon 'monkish humiliation is destructive of all virtue, all energy, all management' (217). For the sensitive task of Minister of Religion, Napoleon chose Jean Portalis, an author of the Civil Code and a pragmatic liberal.

Perhaps most important of all, Napoleon held firmly to his principle of separate temporal and spiritual realms. Despite his dominant authority, he did not subordinate the Church to his temporal power. Although he later dispossessed the Pope of his temporal domains and held him prisoner at Fontainebleau, the Concordat remained in force until 1905

and became the model for 30 similar treaties between Rome
and foreign governments. French churches were once more
opened to worshippers, the religious civil war was ended and a
fresh, independent episcopate appointed. Despite his differences with Napoleon, Pius VII himself pronounced the
Concordat 'a healing act, Christian and heroic' (223).

Andrew Carnegie

The Relentless Builder

Andrew Carnegie's leadership in forging what became the
world's largest and most profitable integrated steel company
in the post-Civil War United States reflected both superior
business acumen and effective leadership skills. While he
espoused a host of worthy values – a commitment to American
democracy and liberal economics, a Chartist belief in workers'
rights, and global pacifism – often these values were subordinated to his relentless, enthusiastic pursuit of building an industrial empire.

Carnegie's business success was rooted in his intuitive understanding of the critical elements for success in building a
major industrial business in the late nineteenth century:
driving costs down by investment in new technology and ruthless operating economies; achieving successful forward and
backward integration, and leveraging his economic power to
dominate the market not only for his own products but also
those of his suppliers and clients. His business philosophy was
well suited to the explosive industrial growth in the US after
the Civil War: 'gain distance by carrying full sail' and 'small
profits and large sales' were typical phrases which flowed from
his frequent letters and speeches.

Accompanying this business philosophy was an equally
dynamic and relentless leadership style. His enthusiasm and
energy for virtually any activity in which he engaged usually
overwhelmed opposition both in the market-place and within
the Carnegie Steel group. Whether repairing damaged bridges
as a young superintendent on the Pennsylvania Railroad,
clearing vital railway routes for Union forces during the Civil

War or seeking out competitor cost data in his eternal search for operating economies, Carnegie drove himself as well as his colleagues. He acknowledged that 'whatever I engage, I must push inordinately' (Wall: 31), and 'I was probably the most inconsiderate superintendent that ever was entrusted with the management of a great property ... for, not knowing fatigue myself, I overworked the men' (149). As the majority stockholder but not a member of the management team or the board of Carnegie Steel, he would insist on receiving detailed board minutes and respond in painful and insistent detail in his much-feared 'thoughts on the Minutes'.

While his determination understandably tended to stifle opposition, he tempered this with sensitivity and insight into the needs of others – whether competitors, suppliers, politicians or his own colleagues. As a skilled negotiator, he successfully bought up competitors and suppliers, leveraged his buying power to negotiate lower supply costs and integrate vertically, and finally sold out to J.P. Morgan at a handsome price reflecting Morgan's desire to cartellize the steel industry. He ran Carnegie Steel as a partnership with himself as the controlling partner but rewarding individual managers with equity which eventually created a host of millionaires. 'Life in the Carnegie kingdom [was] a perpetual race, in which each contestant put forth his final effort, understanding that, at the goal, there was a splendid prize.' (665). Yet he would not drive his own opinions over the united views of his managers, and meritocratic culture generally permeated the firm. He was capable of targeted flattery to motivate valuable colleagues; his General Manager W.P. Shinn was told that 'with you at the helm and my pulling an oar outside, we are bound to put it [Carnegie Steel] at the head of rail-making concerns'. (326).

Although he betrayed his Chartist commitment to labour unions by supporting a lock-out which led to violence at the Homestead plant in 1892, Carnegie had a deft sense of the possible. One of his great talents was 'his sensitive, and most intuitive perceptiveness of the boundaries beyond which one could not step with impunity' (209), whether in labour negotiations, political dealings, management debate or cutting deals with suppliers and clients.

Having sold his controlling interest in Carnegie Steel at the age of 65 to create a massive fortune, Carnegie then commit-

ted himself to a philanthropic vision he had first entertained
at the age of 35. In this totally different environment he
applied the same relentless, thorough and sanguine pursuit of
this objective, with 'Tenacity and steady sailing to the haven
we clear for ... supreme confidence in one's own ideas ... and
above all, placing use above popularity' (805). Yet this endeavour – as in his efforts to influence political forces in the years
before World War I – Carnegie was less successful in driving
change. For one with his energy and determination, philan-
thropy 'would never be enough to absorb his interest completely ... he needed the satisfaction of knowing that he was
manipulating forces and moving men, not just with his check-
book, but also with his ideas' (911).

Any evaluation of Carnegie's leadership must focus on his
success in building a major industrial business but also devot-
ing virtually all the proceeds of its sale to the public welfare –
essentially the founding of universities, public libraries (2811
of them!) and support of students, teachers and others
throughout the world. Yet he must also carry the stigma of enforcing a cost reduction programme which led to violence at
Homestead.

Case-Study: Building a Steel Business

Carnegie's success in building what became the U.S. Steel
Company was his signal achievement as a businessman as well
as a leader of men. In 1872, having made a fortune in the aftermath of the Civil War by financial speculation in a variety of
markets, he decided to centre his efforts on the manufacture
of steel with the construction of the Edgar Thompson mill in
Pittsburgh. While his business acumen and ruthless competitive spirit underpinned the remarkable financial success of
this business, Carnegie's leadership skills also played a central
role in this achievement.

In the realm of business strategy, Carnegie reinforced his
commitment to low-cost production using innovative technology by consistent, hands-on and energetic leadership.
Managers were peppered with reminders of the importance of
the company remaining the low-cost producer, often supplemented by evidence he regularly collected from competitors
by a variety of means. An early proponent of management-by-
walking-around, he plunged deeply into the mill's day-to-day

operations. Having determined that he could slash insurance costs by replacing traditional wooden facilities with steel, he proceeded to do so and cancelled his insurance coverage. Insisting on using the latest technology to drive down costs, he pioneered the use of the open hearth furnace in Pittsburgh. In the 1890s, having delegated operating respons-ibility to his management team and retaining only a seat on the Board as principal stockholder, Carnegie continued to offer detailed advice by correspondence. When a serious re-cession hit in 1873 shortly after the start-up of his first mill, Carnegie retained his self-confidence and travelled to his bankers J.S. Morgan in London, where he successfully raised the necessary finance to carry his new company through the difficult period.

Carnegie also exercised leadership in the selection, motiva-tion and management of his executive team. He insisted on employing the very best specialists and, in most cases, followed their advice. Thus Alexander Holley, the recognized expert in design and construction of blast furnaces, W.P. Shinn from the Allegheny Railroad as general manager, and Captain William Jones as plant superintendent were cajoled, recruited from the competition or otherwise induced to join Carnegie. Henry Phipps was Carnegie's in-house cost-cutter. Having discovered Henry Clay Frick's management skills after buying into his coke business, Carnegie insisted on Frick's taking over Carnegie Steel's management and becoming a major stock-holder. A pioneer in executive compensation, Carnegie offered liberal opportunities for these key men to earn a share of the equity in what had become one of the most profitable enterprises in America. Internal competition was a central feature of his leadership; with four furnaces eventually operat-ing, Carnegie fostered a perpetual race for weekly perform-ance with appropriate financial rewards for the winners. A typical greeting from Carnegie to the winner was 'congratula-tions: what about next week?' While prepared to yield to the arguments of his managers, Carnegie did not hesitate to elim-inate even a general manager such as Shinn who insisted on his own prerogatives.

The same blend of carrot and stick was used with competi-tors, clients and suppliers. The name Edgar Thompson was chosen for his first mill to flatter the eponymous head of the

Pennsylvania Railroad, a major client of the mill. Having joined the Bessemer Steel Association, the elite club of steelmakers who operated a price cartel, Carnegie proceeded to threaten – successfully – to undercut them unless offered a higher market quota. Suppliers like Frick found themselves alternatively bullied to provide better terms and cajoled to sell out to Carnegie in his search for vertical integration.

Carnegie's achievement was to build in 30 years an industrial giant whose return on equity in the 30–40 per cent range fully justified the payment by J.P. Morgan of a fortune which even Carnegie's energy and ambitions could not spend on philanthropic uses. An integral part of this success was due to Carnegie's insight into the motives of his managers, competitors, clients and suppliers and consequent ability to fine-tune the array of material rewards, bullying, flattery and other techniques he used to maximize Carnegie Steel's profitability. Whether addressing a business or human issue, Carnegie was totally consistent throughout his career in his focus on performance in the critical dimensions of cost, innovation and productivity.

Charlemagne

The Benevolent Christian Autocrat

During a 46-year reign which brought together most of present-day Continental Western Europe in the late eighth century AD under his sole leadership, Charlemagne pursued a vision of uniting the Christian world under his paternalistic guidance. While capable of highly unchristian brutality and ruthlessness, he progressively strove to create a moral, well-ordered and efficient theocratic society for his subjects. 'He considered that he had been crowned by God for the sake of the people's welfare, that he was responsible to God for their peace, prosperity and salvation ... under Charles himself benevolence predominated over despotism (Winston: 282).

A leader with a remarkable breadth of talents, Charlemagne's reign was distinguished by military success, a sincere interest in education and the liberal arts, a reforming zeal which penetrated every aspect of society, as well as strong interpersonal skills. 'Like the universal man of the Renaissance, he interested himself in architecture, canal building, music, liturgy, languages, textural criticism of the Bible, poetry, sculpture ... and was also a man of action, and administrator, general and diplomat' (154).

Of central importance to his leadership qualities, however, was an indomitable will – a persistent determination to overcome any opposition to achieve his objectives. Convinced that the neighbouring barbarian Saxon tribes constituted a threat to his Frankish nation, he personally led a 32-year struggle which ultimately, after decades of bloodshed and dislocation, resulted in the incorporation of a Christian Saxon nation in his empire. He would tirelessly criss-cross Europe to put down rebellions, impose his will on independent-minded popes, battle to expand his empire on all its borders, and conduct endless dialogues with his nobles and administrators. The downside of this iron will was a ruthlessness and violent temper when opposed; thus the deportation of thousands of Saxons to the far corners of his Empire and the massacre of 4500 defenceless Saxon warriors at Verden tarnish his Christian record. In the religious domain, in which he treated the Pope as an instrument of his authority, Charles was equally rigorous in his pursuit of heresy. Having instructed himself in the Bible and sacred writings 'he was as capable of writing a book on image worship as he was of delivering a lengthy address on adoptianism to the assembled clergy of the realm at the Frankfurt Council' (224). The outcome was 'a curious medley of democratic and autocratic procedures – with autocracy triumphing in the end' (215).

This overwhelming will-power was usually tempered by a skilled diplomatic sense. Although his authority was never at issue, he was prepared to persuade, to compromise and skilfully to balance opposing functions. During his interminable wars, he could persuade an opposing leader like Widekind or Tassilo to submit to compromise on the issue of religious freedom for pagan Saxons. At home, he mediated between independent-minded nobles and his administrative hierarchy to find the right balance of rights and obligations. To ensure the unity of his empire above regional considerations, he moved his sons and chief administrators from region to region: 'there were no French or Germans in Charles' City of God; there were only fellow members in the Mystical Body of Christ and the practical corpus of Frankish Western Europe' (160). The semi-annual assemblies of the Empire's officers and nobles typified his effective use of the velvet glove and mailed fist: typically he would introduce a proposal for discussion and obtain the views of all concerned, yet retain in classical paternalistic fashion the right of final decision. Meritocracy was also an essential leadership trait. 'He had ignored distinctions of birth and appointed former slaves to hold high office in the state ... he had shifted his bishops and courts around at will, placing Lombards in Neustria, Bavarians in Burgundy' (322).

Charles's leadership repertoire was completed by his administrative skills and total commitment to implementing his vision. Unlike so many other successful commanders, he was a tireless and competent administrator. His totally centralized administrative hierarchy infiltrated every dimension of life in his vast and varied Empire from France through Italy to the eastern borders of the current German state. He was personally involved in the preparation of over a hundred capitularies, or decrees in the religious, moral, economic and other domains. Through his *missi domenici*, or travelling personal emissaries, he imposed loyalty oaths of over forty detailed chapters on his subjects. He even specified the 74 herbs to be grown for his royal gardens. As religious and moral behaviour became an increasing focus of his life, he would bombard his sons and other subjects with a flood of moral directives. To quote his biographer, 'A stream of capitularies ... reveals a Charles whose sense of civic and religious responsibility toward his people ... had become almost obsessional. He admonishes, he exhorts, he preaches.' (285). In the military realm, implementation meant a constant struggle to raise the annual *herrbann* or levy of troops and lead them into battle against neighbouring countries or rebellious provinces. At the age of 62 Charles was still leading his men against the Saxon tribes – delegating responsibility to his generals and sons only when totally satisfied with their loyalty and competence.

His creation of the Holy Roman Empire – culminating in his coronation at St Peter's in Rome in AD800 – was a unique achievement never since repeated in the western world. The weaker leadership skills of his successors produced the patchwork of nations we know today – yet the vision of a unified Christian western Europe has spawned a host of imitators.

What is equally unique in Charles's achievement is the paternalistic vision: a moral life for all citizens in a well-ordered society, as opposed to the more egotistical motives of others who have achieved total power by the sword or the ballot box.

Case-Study: Undermining the Opposition: the Case of Cousin Tassilo

Charlemagne's leadership almost invariably blended force and diplomacy, whether dealing with the Pope, his perpetual rivals the Saxons, or another chieftain who threatened his mastery over Christian Europe.

Tassilo of Bavaria was such a chieftain, and the duel between the two is an excellent case-study in Charlemagne's use of leadership skills to overwhelm the opposition. A contemporary of Charlemagne, Tassilo inherited the neighbouring strategic dukedom of Bavaria and married a sister of Charles's Lombard wife. Intelligent, religious and the heir to a powerful dukedom, Tassilo constituted a clear threat to Charlemagne's ambitions. Having sworn the standard oath of feudal loyalty to his overlord Charlemagne, Tassilo nevertheless ruled independently over a strategic Christian dukedom and relied on shrewdness and diplomacy to retain effective independence from Charlemagne while expanding his dukedom and threatening to ally with Charlemagne's Saxon enemies as well as the Pope.

Charlemagne's initial response was to place diplomatic pressure on Tassilo, whose army's presence in Charlemagne's effort to conquer Spain is probably an indication of this pressure. Charlemagne's influence on the Pope may well have persuaded Tassilo in turn to offer allegiance to Charlemagne at an assembly of the Franks held annually at Worms. To obtain this oath Charlemagne was prepared to submit to the indignity of offering hostages to ensure the safety of Tassilo at Worms, reinforcing his apparent friendship with gifts and goodwill. In 781 Tassilo actually tested Charles's army in a border skirmish and won, as a number of neighbouring states gathered their forces against the Frankish monarch.

To conquer such a well-connected Christian monarch and vassal as Tassilo was not a simple task. Charlemagne started by placing pressure on Tassilo through his influence on the Pope to reach a compromise. At one of the assemblies at Worms, Charles called for an invasion of Bavaria, only to be turned down. In what must be one of few such occasions, his nobles told their Emperor he should give Tassilo another chance by presenting himself in Worms as a vassal. When Tassilo refused, Charlemagne had his excuse and marched on Bavaria. Yet no physical force was necessary as Charlemagne's allies in the Church threatened anathema on Tassilo, who found himself deserted by his nobles. Thus in 787 Tassilo capitulated and offered allegiance to Charlemagne. Once again Charlemagne showered his cousin with gifts and friendliness – with a weather eye on the accompanying Bavarian nobles whom he was courting.

The last act in the drama took place the following year at Ingleheim at an assembly of all the empire's nobles. Tassilo and his family were seized and subjected to a classical show trial by his Bavarian peers but orchestrated by Charlemagne. Having seen the futility of resistance, Tassilo confessed his treason and was sentenced to death. Once again the diplomatic face of Charlemagne appeared, as Tassilo was sent to a nearby monastery at St Goar for the rest of his life – reappearing six years later to support Charlemagne at the Council of Frankfurt for a church synod. In the meantime Bavaria was speedily incorporated into the Frankish state.

Thus Charlemagne had once again demonstrated his technique of dealing with rivals – described by his biographer as one 'which consisted in alternate leniency and severity, in successive or sometime simultaneous displays of the velvet glove and the mailed fist' (181).

Oliver Cromwell

A Successful Military Leader Struggles in the Political Domain

As the political battle in mid-seventeenth century England between King and people reached a crisis point, Oliver Cromwell's remarkable military skills propelled him into political prominence following the execution of King Charles I. Undefeated in battle, he spent the five years of his

Protectorate until his death balancing the conflicting forces of the Royalists, the army, Scottish Presbyterians, populist Levellers and a host of religious minorities.

To address this kaleidoscope of conflict, Cromwell articulated and lived a vision of a godly England. Determined to do God's will, which he saw reflected in events such as the outcome of military battles, Cromwell 'had a continuing obsession with his self-ordained task of bringing about a more godly state in England' (Fraser: 587). His personal values reflected this vision in terms of a compassionate, conciliatory approach which continually sought out the reasonable middle ground, whether it be the Putney debates with his army colleagues, negotiations with King Charles, quelling mutinies of underpaid soldiers, debating with populist Levellers or parliamentary opponents, or negotiating with the Scottish leaders. As one contemporary put it, 'By courteous overtures to cajole and charm all parties when he goes about a doubtful service' (Fraser: 362). Another commented that 'No man knew more of men' (702).

Yet his greatest leadership skills were on the battlefield. A self-taught soldier who created the disciplined New Model Army, his brilliance was based on boldness, confidence in his disciplined forces, and decisiveness. He was 'always at his best when the situation called for precipitate and decisive action' (195). Drawn by events and the absence of alternative leadership following the death of Charles I to become effectively the head of government, he painfully groped his way toward what he felt was God's will. He was described as 'A man hoping to talk his way through to truth' (213). Once outside the military domain, however, indecision was often the product of the violent political forces buffeting his government. He thus took over two months to decide to refuse the crown offered by the Army and was unable in his final years to name a successor. At the same time, he was capable of violent rages when he felt betrayed – hence the anger and violence of his repeated dissolution of Parliamentary bodies whom he could not persuade to follow his lead. He is recorded as having told the recalcitrant body 'it is you that have forced me to do this, for I have sought the Lord night and day that he could strengthen me' (421).

Cromwell's efforts to create an alternative political base did not survive his death and the subsequent restoration of

Charles II. Arguably his personal vision of a godly England was
not sufficient to build the broad base of support needed to
provide an alternative to the Stuart line. While enjoying a high
degree of personal stature and respect, Cromwell was repeatedly unable to weld a base of support either in the nation as a
whole or in a series of parliaments summoned during the
1650s.

Case-Study: Seeking the Middle Way in 1647

Throughout Cromwell's military and political leadership he
sought the rational middle course. In 1646–7, a lull in the Civil
War obliged Cromwell to turn his hand to leadership off the
battlefield. His efforts during this difficult period to reconcile
Parliament, the Army he had helped to create, and King
Charles epitomize Cromwell's talent for leadership in conflict.

Have returned from his successful military career in 1646,
Cromwell as a leader of the Independents in Parliament had
fallen into a state of depression over the conflict which raged
among the three power centres. Angry unpaid soldiers; an un-
sympathetic Parliament dominated by the Presbyterian
faction, and a King held prisoner by Parliament and determined to exploit differences between the two – all created a
potent brew of conflict. Cromwell was delegated by Parliament
to negotiate at Saffron Walden with the army which,
Parliament proposed, was to be disbanded. Threatened with
arrest by an increasingly suspicious Parliament, Cromwell fled
London to throw his lot in with the army. Joining the army's
leadership, he took a middle path in negotiating a settlement
with Charles which might have succeeded had not Charles
been playing a double game with his Scottish supporters.
Cromwell resisted the demands of the left-wing agitators in the
army to march on London and apply force to Parliament,
saying 'that which you have as force I look upon as nothing'
(202). When the left-wing mob took over London, however,
he led his regiment into the City to restore order.

There ensued an extended period of negotiations in which
Cromwell moved from being a successful military leader to
become an increasingly skilled political negotiator. On one occasion he posted his men near the House of Commons to
ensure that the Null and Void ordinance was passed to repeal
the acts of the former House. As the undisputed leader of the

army, Cromwell took the lead in attempting to negotiate a settlement with Charles based on the proposals of the heads of the army. At the same time he argued against the army's left-wing agitators and Levellers who, threatening mutiny, proposed total popular sovereignty. Aware of his unpopularity, he points out in one of his letters that: 'we doubt not but God will clear our integrity and innocency from any other end we aim at but his glory and the public good' (210).

In this charged atmosphere, the army debates began in Putney, one of the most extraordinary conclaves in English history. As president of the meeting, Cromwell spoke forcefully but in a rambling and obscure mode which his biographers attributed to his genuine doubts on the way forward. Torn between the demands of the Levellers for revolution and the traditionalist view presented by his son-in-law Henry Ireton, he gave the appearance of agreeing with both sides. As opinion on the Army Council swung to the left, Cromwell was also aware of rumours that Charles was plotting to escape and was the target of left-wing assassins. Charles's subsequent escape and imprisonment on the Isle of Wight evoked Cromwell's joy to the extent that it has been suggested that Cromwell played a role in the escape as part of his 'new political practice of leading, cajoling and suggesting where he could not drive' (Fraser: 223).

There is no doubt, however, of Cromwell's role in the first rendezvous designed to transmit the Army Council's decision to the troops. Confronted at Corkbush Field in November 1647 with several rebellious regiments, a furious Cromwell drew his sword, seized the ringleaders and had one shot. At the same time in his 'perpetual balancing act' he disassociated himself from the Leveller tendency in the army.

His balancing act ceased a few days later with his decision against any settlement with the King – presumably driven by discovery of incontrovertible evidence of Charles's double dealing with the Scots and Presbyterians. Under his leadership, the House of Commons voted not to have any future communications with the King. Within a few months, the Second Civil War was under way with Cromwell leading his army to South Wales.

Thus another period of difficult political leadership alternated in Cromwell's life with a military conflict where his battlefield skills ensured success. Cromwell was to have many more such challenges when he was pitted against powerful forces to the left and right. Although the laurels of a peace-maker in this turbulent transition period were more difficult to win than those of victorious general, Cromwell stubbornly continued to seek the middle path until his death.

Charles de Gaulle

The Leader as Embodiment of the Nation

From his days as a rebellious officer at the collapse of France in 1940 through the military revolt over Algeria in the 1950s and student unrest in 1968, Charles de Gaulle successfully faced conflict. He addressed it with a simple but uncompromising vision of the authority and legitimacy of the French nation which he alone was equipped to embody and interpret. His leadership role ceased when that nation, through his chosen vehicle of the referendum, denied him this legitimacy in 1968.

De Gaulle's vision was that of the eternal, legitimate French nation whose leader – himself – held untrammelled authority above political movements and current events. Whether it be the Vichy government, the rebellious French generals in 1958, the French communist party or Allied governments, the inter-ests of the French nation, with himself as their interpreter, must be sustained. Internationally, the vision called for France at the core of a Europe plotting its own course between rival superpowers. His own role, in the view of his biographer Lacouture, was 'above political struggles, a national arbiter, elected by citizens holding a public mandate (Lacouture, 1991: 196). In this view, 'all human activity is ordered around the nation ... and led by a hero.'

Implementing this vision required primarily an appeal for firmness of purpose to sustain the legitimate authority. Thus his call to arms in June 1940 against the German invader, the elimination of independent militias in 1944, the appeal in 1958 to the army to support the legitimate government and the constant theme of the subsequent referenda which he used to resolve domestic issues. For a decade after reassuming power in 1958, his blend of realism and vision served to bolster the economy, strengthen the franc and resolve the conflict over Algeria. Only when his will failed him in 1968, following the student violence, did his leadership falter: Lacouture describes 'a man usually so firm in extraordinary circumstances ... was seen to be confused, hesitant, passing from the temptation to resign to a determination to stamp out chaos' (527).

His firmness of purpose was tempered, depending on the circumstances, by skill in compromise. While insistent to his allies in wartime on France's presumed authority, when assuming political power in both 1944 and 1958 he took care to sustain continuity through retaining a broad range of views in his new cabinets. Faced with possible civil war over the Algerian crisis, he skilfully retained support from both the rebellious military and the democratic forces in France until he could negotiate, three years later, the self-determination he knew was inevitable. Ambiguity in effect became one of his strongest weapons: termed by one of his Cabinet as the 'Prince of equivocation' (263), he acknowledged in 1958: 'I must be seen as the man of reconciliation and not as the champion of one of the factions' (172).

His communications skills were largely those of the orator. While he enjoyed his '*bain de foule*', plunging physically into an enthusiastic crowd, he made his greatest impact with the electorate by his skilfully-crafted set speeches. With his colleagues in government, the dialogue was minimal; de Gaulle dominated cabinet meetings as well as loyal prime ministers like Michel Debré and Georges Pompidou.

As a committed democrat responsive to the will of the electorate, de Gaulle renounced power in 1946 when obliged to work with an antagonistic Parliament under the existing Constitution – only to return in 1958 when he could mobilize the votes to ensure presidential hegemony. With France in conflict again in 1968, he insisted on another referendum – albeit on subjects of minor importance – to reaffirm his mandate. After a decade in power and at the age of 78, he was reduced to threatening his retirement as the principal argument for support, telling a colleague: 'I want to plunge the French people into doubt and anxiety in order to regain control of the situation.' (552) Whereas he could mobilize majority support on past issues such as Algeria and the personal presidency, the absence of an equivalent issue plus a general sense of his loss of authority in 1968 produced a negative response and precipitated de Gaulle's immediate retirement.

Case-Study: Resolving the Algerian Crisis in 1958

Charles de Gaulle's deft assumption of power in 1958, blending masterful ambiguity with a deep understanding of his followers' motives and firm adherence to his basic principles, is a classic leadership case-study for the twentieth century. He faced two apparently irreconcilable views: the French army in Algeria determined to replace what it viewed as a spineless government, and the widespread opposition among the domestic French political forces, led by the communists and socialists, against an overthrow of constitutional processes. How de Gaulle first reconciled these views to obtain power, and then used this power to restore consensus in a divided country, merits close examination.

As the Algerian crisis loomed in early 1958 with the army threatening to take power from the French civil authorities, de Gaulle publicly announced his support for an independent Algeria. At the same time, he confirmed his long-standing commitment to an army which obeyed its political masters. When asked how he would reconcile these principles in the face of an army disobeying the civilian government and taking power in Algeria in the name of colonial France, he shrouded himself in ambiguity, saying to his colleague Delbecque in Algiers 'I will know how to reconcile my responsibilities' (163).

While de Gaulle remained aloof from the increasingly intense discussions between Paris and Algiers, his loyal lieutenants – Debré, Soustelle, Chaban-Delmas, Guichard and Foccart – in the two capitals both gathered support for de Gaulle's return and transmitted messages which gave both opposing sides reason to believe de Gaulle supported their point of view. When the French army under General Massu took power in Algiers on 13 May, Massu thus publicly supported a Gaullist government in Paris.

In Paris, de Gaulle responded by an enigmatic declaration that he was prepared to assume power – without even mentioning Algiers. To the press, he talked of being the arbitrator in the national interest and announcing that he would make contact with the rebellious generals. Convinced they had de Gaulle's support, the generals prepared to launch a military take-over in Paris, cancelling the operation only when President Coty announced on 29 May his willingness to meet de Gaulle with the intention of forming a government of national safety.

With the President's support, de Gaulle made his historic return to the National Assembly to request full powers and approval of constitutional change – in effect the death of the fourth Republic. In the words of Henri Guillemin, 'the Gaullist strategy consisted of allowing the political class to see the threat of violence and therefore to side with him, and to let the soldiers believe that he was their man' (176). Before the National Assembly on 1 June, having formed a government primarily taken from the existing political establishment, de Gaulle posed the principal issue of the granting of constituent powers – basically a new constitution which was to be submitted to a referendum. His appeal was to the Assembly's trust in him to resolve the Algerian crisis and approve the delegation of constitutional powers. While democrats like François Mitterrand and Pierre Mendes-France voted against him, de Gaulle easily won the necessary three-fifths majority vote.

Having won power in Paris by constitutional means, de Gaulle immediately turned to the clear challenge of the army in Algeria. Once again, clear principles were blended with ambiguity. He responded to his reception in Algiers by a delirious crowd on 4 June by greeting them with the ambiguous phrase '*je vous ai compris*' (I have understood you) followed by a reference to a single college of government involving the entire people of Algeria, both the French minority and Algerian majority. Acknowledging privately to his son-in-law that he had avoided committing himself to '*Algérie française*' (an Algeria dominated by the French) he spoke of a 'most French solution'. In what was perhaps an involuntary mis-step before another emotional crowd in Mostanagem, he did mention the symbolic phrase *Algérie française* the next day, and returned to Paris having gained the support of the army, marginalized the extremists, and held out to the native Algerians the prospect of eventual control of their country.

In a few short weeks, de Gaulle had avoided a military take-over, won power by constitutional means, and lanced the Algerian boil. Political opposition from the left and an extremist right-wing military faction would harass him in the coming years, but his achievement in 1958 was a lasting one as he stabilized the currency, brought his army to heel, and launched France on a period of economic growth and political stability.

Mohandas Gandhi

The Struggle for Truth through Sacrifice

Rarely has a leader exercised effective power for decades in a major nation without a political or military infrastructure beneath him. Mohandas Gandhi achieved this unique leadership role in India in the twentieth century by propagating and living a vision of truth through sacrifice, with truth defined as a community living in peace, respecting the rights of all its members, and relying on its own efforts to support itself. Confronted with the inevitable opposition and likely violence, he accepted the need for sacrifice, including that of his own life.

As his vision evolved during his defence of human rights in South Africa and India, Gandhi's moral influence grew – not only with the groups he defended but also with the governmental authorities he challenged. Not only could he accept imprisonment, and mobilize millions to march for peace but his total commitment to sacrifice himself to his *satyagraha*, or truth force, obliged governments to offer concessions which ultimately led to India's independence in 1947. As Robert Payne puts it, he had 'extraordinary power to dominate any situation, his senses reaching out until he had made everyone his willing accomplice' (Payne, 1969: 231). Moreover, 'He dreamt of assembling a small army of dedicated men, issuing stern commands, and leading them to some almost unobtainable goal' (301).

An essential component of his leadership was a superhuman level of energy throughout his life-span of 78 years. In his last years, his daily routine involved writing perhaps 60 letters, receiving dozens of visitors, running prayer meetings, and spinning at his wheel – as well as constantly organizing and leading pilgrimages, resistance movements and political representations. In the ashrams he set up in South Africa and India for his followers, 'he was not only the Prime Minister ... he was also the chief judge, the chief sanitary inspector, the chief teacher, the chief baker and marmalade maker' (231).

With this total personal commitment came an equally total demand on others, often expressed in tyranny over his own family and close associates. Having made up his mind on an action plan, he could not be moved: 'in matters of conscience I am uncompromising. Nobody can make me yield' (351). He was also quoted as saying 'I put far too heavy burdens on people' (269), and 'I hesitate to ask others to do things which I cannot do myself' (186).

Gandhi also totally lived his vision. For a variety of causes – Hindu–Muslim collaboration, the rights of Untouchables, non-discriminatory taxes, and peace after Indian independence – he undertook a remarkable total of 15 fasts, each of which could theoretically last until his death. He wrote, 'The contemplated step is not a method, it is part of my being' (435). Committed to setting an example to Indians of personal cleanliness, he insisted on cleaning latrines both in the ashram and on his travels. When Indians did not live up to his standards, he fasted for them as a form of penance.

The final dimension of his leadership was a complete absence of fear, rooted in the conviction that personal sacrifice was an integral part of the search for truth. In South Africa he was physically assaulted on several occasions without diminishing his willingness to continue the struggle. As the storm clouds grew in pre-independence India he acknowledged that, while he could not prevent a violent partition, he had to be prepared to die for his vision. Confronted by rioting Hindus in 1946, he stated 'I never submit to force of any kind whatsoever' (535). In addition, 'I should love, above all, to fade out doing my duty with my last breath' (526).

The power of his vision – and his total commitment to living it – enabled Gandhi to mobilize millions – whether to march to the sea against a salt tax, to uphold the rights of indigo farmers, to limit civil strife or open Hindu temples to *harijans*

(Untouchables). In Payne's view, there was 'no limit to the power of a pure man fighting for absolute truth' (257).

Yet Gandhi acknowledged the limits of his leadership. In South Africa his efforts to maintain minority rights were overshadowed by the dominance of the white government. He had to acknowledge his inability to sway the Muslim leader Mohammad Ali Jinnah from his commitment to partition in 1947. Above all, he was unable to control the violence of others – which ultimately led to his assassination by Hindu extremists. His only solution was a personal one: he and his *satyagraha* followers could only uphold truth and suffer the personal consequences. He was quoted as saying 'I seek my peace in the storm' (578). 'I want to avoid violence … [but] what is raging within my breast [is to] run the maddest risk which a sane man can run.' (364)

Case-Study: Confronting Communal Violence

Civil strife between Muslims and Hindus in 1946–48 was Gandhi's last – and ultimately fatal – leadership challenge. Now in his mid-seventies, he had successfully achieved compromises with the Boer government in South Africa and the British Raj in India, but civil war in the aftermath of the partition of independent India and Pakistan in 1947 represented the most irreconcilable schism he had faced.

Having been unable to persuade the Muslim leader Jinnah to remain part of India, Gandhi at the age of 77 was in a state of despair with no solution to offer other than an appeal to both sides for *ahimsa*, or communal peace between Hindus and Muslims. Yet he felt he had no choice but to throw all his energies into the struggle for peace. In October 1946 he set off for Noakhali in East Bengal, the site of the first massacre – this time of Hindus by Muslims. Plunging into the centre of the troubled area, Gandhi went from village to village preaching peace and mutual understanding, posting his colleagues in individual villages to keep the peace. He then repeated the process in Bihar, where Hindus had massacred Muslims. Throughout, his message was the same: both sides were to admit their guilt and promise him never to raise their hands again against innocent members of the other community.

Exhausted by the physical and mental pressure, he nevertheless headed back across the subcontinent to East Bengal, where news reached him of new bloodshed there. On the way, he was persuaded to stop in Calcutta where the Muslim minority was threatened with violence by Hindu extremists. He consented to stay in Calcutta only if he could live in the same house with the Muslim leader Suhrawardy. Installed in a devastated Muslim quarter in August 1947 they would live together – or die at the hands of armed Hindu gangs. The house was immediately besieged by furious Hindu youths who accused Gandhi of favouring the Muslim side. He quieted them down by confirming his Hindu credentials and assuring them that he was prepared to stay in the face of their threats without calling for help. One Hindu gang member was quoted as saying 'God knows the old man is a wizard – everyone is won over by him' (535). The crowds gathered the next day and were placated only by Gandhi and Suhrawardy appearing together and Suhrawardy acknowledging that he was responsible for an earlier massacre. The day ended with a peace march orchestrated by Gandhi of 10 000 Muslims and Hindus. On Independence Day, Gandhi's fear of future violence prevented him from sharing the joy of his countrymen who applauded him as Father of the Nation. Governor General Mountbatten congratulated him saying 'In the Punjab we have 55 000 soldiers and large scale rioting on our hands. In Bengal [Calcutta] our forces consist of one man, [Gandhi] and there is no rioting' (538).

A few days later, the right-wing Hindu Mahasabha gathered during the night at his home and awoke the exhausted Gandhi, who had maintained his heavy schedule of writing, interviews and visits despite the surrounding turmoil. Once again he confronted them, encouraging them to kill him, and would have plunged into the crowd if not restrained.

Struggling to find an answer to the dilemma of the civil war, Gandhi decided to commence another fast for peace in an effort to reach out to the men of violence. The rioting continued as Gandhi reconciled himself to death – through violence or fasting. After four days, during which deputations of Hindus, Muslims and Sikhs all pleaded with him to end his fast, assuming his death would provide even greater violence, the riots subsided. Gandhi ended the fast in September 1947 after officials from the various factions signed a paper promising – on their lives – to keep the peace in Calcutta.

A few months later he was dead, assassinated by Hindu extremists while communicating the same message in strife-torn Delhi. Communal hatred was indeed too powerful even for Gandhi's magnetic leadership. Yet his work in Calcutta had demonstrated that a leader totally committed to a vision of peace, willing to offer his life for this vision, and able to be totally fair minded to both factions could interrupt, at least for a time, the violence around him.

Henri de Navarre

Tolerance and Firmness Resolve a Bitter Civil War

In the second half of the sixteenth century, a series of weak Valois monarchs was unable to halt a murderous civil war between the Catholic majority and Protestant minority which devastated France for decades. By positioning himself as a tolerant chief of state above religious factions and acting in the interest of the French nation as a whole, Henri IV of France and Navarre was able to knit together the warring parties and bring to the country a degree of peace and prosperity rare in a century of strife.

Leading 'a weary life between recalcitrant Catholics and suspicious Protestants', he committed himself wholly to the task: 'since God brought me into the world for this Kingdom and not for me, all my senses and efforts are employed only for its advancement and conservation' (Castelot, 1986: 354). In the battle for power among Valois factions, he refused to make war on his predecessor Henri III, supporting him as the legitimate monarch against the Catholic League.

Tolerance was a vital dimension of his vision of the state. 'Those who follow their conscience are of my religion, and I follow all of those who are brave and good.' (106). 'You cannot distinguish between Catholics and Huguenots. Both must be good Frenchmen. I am the King-shepherd who does not want to spill the blood of his sheep' (202).

Yet Henri could only realize this vision through victory on the battlefield, and his boldness and personal bravery were central to his remarkable string of military victories against overwhelming odds. On the battlefield at Coutras, Arques, Cahors, Fontaine Française and Ivry, he regularly attacked enemy forces a multiple of his own in size, invariably leading personally from the front wearing his white-plumed helmet. Cautioned by his faithful Sully to become a less visible target, he replied that 'since it is for my glory and my crown that I fight, my life and everything else ought to be of no consideration with me. This is my fixed resolve' (Hurst, 1937: 92). Acknowledging that he could not guarantee the payment of his troops, he still sent word to his commanders: 'mount your horse, put on your cuirasse, come find your King' (Castelot: 321). Leading a few hundred men against the Spanish army at Fontaine Française, he shouted 'follow me; do what you see me do' (299).

A second dimension of Henri IV's leadership was a personal tolerance and generosity consistent with the vision he held out to the French nation. Reared as a child in the Protestant faith and witness to the barbarous slaughter of his fellow Huguenots at the St Barthelémy massacre in 1572, he nevertheless was prepared not only to abjure his faith for the benefit of national reconciliation but also pardoned Catholic leaders like the Duc de Mayenne against whom he had fought for decades.

At the core of his personal magnetism to both soldiers and civilians was his unfailing humanity and good nature: Hurst notes that 'Navarre maintained an even temper, a constant gaiety, a never-failing toleration, a light-hearted courage, an honesty of purpose, and a thoroughly unfashionable humanity that made him unique in his time' (Hurst: 29). He mixed happily with his subjects both on the battlefield and the streets of Paris. During military campaigns, he slept on the ground under the stars, and in battle was often to be found fighting shoulder to shoulder with his infantrymen.

Yet Henri's humanity was blended with the determination and persistence needed to enforce national reconciliation after decades of violent conflict. Following his assumption of the crown in 1589 after Henri III's assassination, he painstakingly rebuilt the national army and only entered Paris five years later having renounced Protestantism and ensured the support of the great mass of French Catholics. Having crafted the Edict of Nantes as the centrepiece of his policy of freedom of conscience, he spent several years cajoling and threatening the various legislative bodies to endorse it: 'I will cut at the roots of your factions, and as for preachers of sedition, I will cut off their heads ... I love the Catholic religion more than you do, and am more Catholic than you ... I want to be obeyed. It is time that all, drunken with war, become wise' (Castelot: 327).

Blended with these powerful qualities was a passionate and sensual nature which at times threatened Henri's leadership role. Throughout his life he demanded a romantic and sexual relationship with a series of women whose beauty caught his eye. As one foreign ambassador put it, 'this seigneur goes everywhere (in a battle), wants to know everything, exposes himself to all the dangers. And, in the evening, he is still capable of making love' (240). Reputed to be the father of 11 bastard children from over 60 open non-marital relationships, Henri was frequently diverted from his leadership vision by these passions as well as the machinations of his mistresses and their supporters in search of power. Thanks to Sully's frequent interventions – including dissuading Henri from marrying Gabrielle d'Estrées – the damage to the national interest was limited.

Henri's assassination in 1610 – on the eve of war with the Habsburg Emperor, triggered at least in part by the latter's refusal to release Henri's latest paramour – brought to an end a brief period when the French King and his able adviser, the Duc de Sully, reconstructed the French economy after the religious reconciliation. However, within the next century his successors had not only abandoned his policy of tolerance but also exhausted France in a series of wars of aggression.

Case-Study: *Le Saut perilleux* – Abjuring the Protestant Faith a Second Time

Central to Henri IV's efforts to unite his countrymen was his personal religious faith. Brought up in a Catholic court with a fiercely Protestant mother, Henri was forced to renounce his Protestantism amid the slaughter of Protestants at the St Barthelémy in Paris in 1572.

Later, as the leader of the Protestant forces against the Duc de Guise and the Catholic League, the assassination of Guise raised the question once again of his religion. Henri refused to give in, saying, 'what would those who consider me courageous say if I gave up, shamefully, the way I have served God

since the day of my birth … no, it would never befit the King
of Navarre even if there were 30 crowns to win.' (184)

Yet the assassination in 1589 of King Henri III, who named
him as his successor, raised the question once again. Henri IV
stood on his principles and hoped to win over the Catholic
majority by appeals to political unity as well as force of arms.
But after Henri III's death the majority of the royal army
melted away from his leadership, and he was forced to retreat
from Paris. With only a few thousand troops and holding only
one-sixth of France, the new king was obliged to win back his
kingdom on the battlefield.

The battle of Arques was won against the Catholic Duc de
Mayenne who outnumbered Henri's army by over four to one.
He marched on Paris and won the battle of Ivry in 1590, but
his siege of Paris was lifted by Spanish forces supporting the
Catholic army. With the great mass of Frenchmen clamouring
for peace, the Catholic League opened negotiations with
Henri. He tried to reassure both Catholics and Protestants of
his peaceful intentions without changing his faith: 'You have
no reason to be alarmed … I enter the house not to stay there
but to clean it up … pray for me and I will love you' (253).

But his religion remained the only issue blocking a peaceful
settlement. The Catholic majority insisted on his conversion,
while his Huguenot allies demanded he remain faithful to his
mother's religion. To them he protested 'if I followed your
opinion, there would soon be neither king nor kingdom in
France. I want to give peace to all my subjects and rest for my
soul' (253).

In May 1593, he decided to repudiate Protestantism a
second time – the *'saut perilleux'*, a true leap of faith in several
respects. The leap was a resounding success. The French
clergy swung to his side after the necessary theological argu-
mentation; he was crowned in Chartres, and he finally entered
Paris in 1594 to subdue without bloodshed the foreign mercenaries who had held the capital. In keeping with his commitment, he offered an amnesty to the League and swore loyalty
to the Catholic religion, saying 'I confess that my victory
comes to me from God … unworthy as I am. As he has pardoned me, so I want to pardon others, forgetting the weaknesses of my people, in showing myself more forgiving … than
I ever was' (282).

Thus five years after inheriting the crown from the dying Henri III, his successor was able to win over both his capital and the hearts of the majority of his countrymen. Whatever his personal views on the merits of the two religions, Henri IV made his great leap to bring the French nation together. By waiting until he was clearly the dominant military force, he was able to make the religious conversion from a position of strength as opposed to the situation in 1589.

Henri IV's unswerving pursuit of a united country, combined with his military genius, thus finally enabled him to make the choice which he had dreaded since the prospect of the French Crown appeared. While religious conflict continued in France after his conversion, the country enjoyed under the balance of his reign a period of relative political peace and economic prosperity.

Adolf Hitler

A Vision of National Renewal Ends in National Disaster

Adolf Hitler's vision of German nationalistic renewal and fulfilment – a Thousand-Year Reich with himself as supreme leader – found a strong response in a Germany frustrated by defeat in World War I, beset by economic problems and bereft of strong political leadership under the Weimar Republic. More remarkable than this ambitious vision, however, was Hitler's ability to achieve it – rising in a decade from a demagogic orator in an obscure fringe party to the respected and unchallenged leader who, by a succession of bold manoeuvres, had achieved an unparalleled dominance of the European continent by mid-1941.

Yet the effort to complete this vision by conquering living-space in Russia for the German nation proved one gamble too many. The resulting collapse of the vision revealed its total identification with Hitler's own pursuit of personal power rather than the true interests of the nation.

This vision – including its less noble attacks on scapegoats in the form of Slavs, Jews and communists – was fully articulated in *Mein Kampf,* written by Hitler in prison in 1924 following his failed 1923 *putsch* in Munich. His legal ascent to power in 1933 – and rapid consolidation thereafter – was a product of Hitler's unique ability to appeal to the emotions of a nation and his equally remarkable exercise of will-power and single-minded pursuit of this vision for the two decades after composing *Mein Kampf.*

Hitler's charismatic appeal as an orator was rooted in a well-articulated, intuitive understanding of mass psychology. His quotations in *Mein Kampf* and elsewhere reflect a deep understanding of human motivation, which Hitler was able to turn to his own benefit rather than that of his audience. For example: 'The masses are a resource to be mobilized, not to be represented. The art of leadership consists in concentrating the attention of the people on a single adversary' (Bullock, 1991: 466). 'To be a leader means to be able to move the masses' (80). 'The psychology of the broad masses is accessible only to what is strong and uncompromising' (86).

As his contemporary Otto Strasser put it, 'Hitler responds to the vibrations of the human heart with the delicacy of a seismograph enabling him ... to act as a loudspeaker proclaiming the most secret desires, the least admissible instincts, the sufferings and personal revolts of a whole nation' (397). While his dramatic outpourings and fits of temper might give the appearance of loss of control, Hitler's public performances were carefully scripted with an eye to the audience, whether a rally in a beer hall or negotiations with a British prime minister.

This talent was placed at the service of an iron will, a conviction in the correctness of his vision which did not desert Hitler until his suicide in 1945. Integral to the vision was a will to power in a Darwinian struggle in which only the strong-willed would survive. This supreme effort of will carried Hitler through the failure of his 1923 *putsch*; frustrating years of building the Nazi party; 28 months of negotiations with the Weimar leadership to achieve a peaceful, legal assumption of power; maintaining a delicate balance between his revolutionary followers in the Stormtroopers (SA) and the conservative bastions of traditional German society, and finally the series of military defeats after 1941. Hitler truly lived up to his boast; 'I shall shrink from nothing and destroy everyone who is opposed to me. I shall never survive the defeat of my people.

No capitulation to the forces without; no revolution from within' (719).

Hitler's blend of boldness, self-confidence and intuition regularly upset the calculations of his adversaries. Von Papen, who supported his candidacy for Chancellor in 1933, replied to his critics saying there was 'no danger at all. We've hired him for our act' (283). Constantly overruled by Hitler, the German generals were either out-shouted by him, dismissed, or embarrassed by his successes in such bold initiatives as the attack on Norway or the invasion of France in 1940 through the Ardennes. Having achieved power, Hitler was ruthless in exercising it – whether in the 1934 SA purge or the elimination of the European Jews.

Yet Hitler's leadership ultimately failed as a result of his over-confidence – the product of a succession of brilliant but unexpected victories between 1933 and 1940 – and his unwillingness to manage the nation on a sustained basis with the help of experienced subordinates. By temperament and conviction, Hitler viewed himself as the leader whose inspiration both set the objectives and permitted him to overrule those implementing the vision. As one of his generals pointed out, 'The Fuhrer was interested in the very big issues and also the tiniest details. Anything in between did not interest him' (639). Thus the Thousand-Year Reich collapsed after the misjudgement of attacking Russia in 1941 and the series of disastrous orders given subsequently by Hitler overruling his generals.

Case-Study: Winning Power by Democratic Means

Hitler's assumption of power by democratic means between the 1930 election and his nomination as Chancellor in 1933 is a classic study in disciplined focus on a single objective, the skilful manipulation of key constituencies, and a successful appeal to the emotions of the broad electorate.

With 19 per cent of the popular vote and a second place in the 1930 elections, Hitler needed to win over the conservative German army command and the politicians who influenced President Hindenberg as well as demonstrate greater electoral strength – at the same time as retaining his SA Brownshirts whose street violence and revolutionary views threatened to undermine Hitler's avowed appeal to tradition and the democratic process. All this was to be achieved without an economic and political programme other than an emotional appeal for national renewal and against the enemies of the German people. Hitler first mobilized Goebbels' electoral machine whose mass rallies featuring Hitler's emotional appeals doubled the Nazis' vote in three elections to garner 37 per cent of the vote as the largest single party. The Nazi party had thus successfully won the support of a broad-based coalition of Protestants, pensioners, rural and small-town voters to whom Hitler's appeal for national renewal was particularly compelling.

Concurrently, over a 28-month period Hitler engaged in delicate negotiations with the leading power brokers close to President von Hindenberg, von Papen and von Schleicher, to trade his electoral support for participation in a strong government able to address Germany's economic problems. When centrist politicians such as Bruning were unable to implement tough economic measures, Hindenberg's kingmakers turned to more extremist leaders like Hitler. Using 'calculated ambiguity' as to his goals, Hitler hung tenaciously to his demand to be named Chancellor. At the same time he was aware that his electoral support might have peaked. Nevertheless he continued to negotiate until von Papen, confident that he could control Hitler, arranged for his selection by Hindenberg as Chancellor in January 1933.

At the same time Hitler had to keep his own troops in line. Brutal mob violence by SA gangs threatened to cost Hitler precious votes and tarnish his democratic credentials. The angry resignation of his second in command and head of Party Organization, Gregor Strasser, sent shock waves through the Nazi organization. But Hitler quickly restructured the party, placed loyal subordinates in key positions, and presented a unified front to the outside world.

Within six months of his assuming the Chancellorship, Hitler had taken effective power by unleashing a reign of terror and removing the constitutional barriers imposed on him. His virtuoso performance in 1930–3 was driven by a single-minded determination to win the Chancellorship by patient negotiations, supported by the use of the mailed fist and his electoral clout. On occasions he would overplay his hand in negotiating the power game, but in January 1933 the rivalry among Hindenberg's lieutenants gave him the title he could not win by an electoral majority.

Isabella la Catolica

The Vision of a United, Christian Nation

Grasping the leadership of Castile following 50 years of civil strife, political fragmentation and weak kingship, Isabella of Castile in the late fifteenth century imposed on her subjects her vision of a unified and powerful Castilian state propagating a pure, fundamental Christianity. While this vision produced one of the most cruel and enduring religious persecutions of Western history, any scruples she may have had 'were subsumed by a greater duty ... [her] commitment to make Castile one nation united by the purity of the Christian faith', in the words of Nancy Rubin (Rubin, 1991: 303).

Isabella's leadership was marked above all by her extraordinary will-power in implementing the vision. As a child she was a pawn in the constant battle between her brother King Enrique and his independent-minded grandees. For years her inheritance was under scrutiny and the subject of fluctuating political currents. Yet she fought against arranged marriages she regarded as inconsistent with Castilian interests and ultimately married Ferdinand of neighbouring Aragon despite her brother's opposition. Having been crowned Queen on the latter's death, she imposed her will on Ferdinand by retaining political control of Castile while Ferdinand's military prowess was employed largely in extending Castilian borders rather than those of Aragon. Fully capable of jumping onto a horse for an extended night ride to enforce her commands, she was also able to confront an angry mob in Segovia demanding: 'my vassals and my servants, tell me what you desire, for if it is for the good of my city and kingdom, I want it too' (153). In the battle of wills with Enrique over his succession, she dominated him 'through the sheer force of her will; her forbearance overcame his restlessness, her determination bested his indecision' (120). The outcome was impressive: 'the trust she inspired among her subjects became the cornerstone of a new national identity – one enabling her to consolidate royal power, codify the Castilian laws, administer justice, conquer the Moors, and support visionaries like Christopher Columbus' (6).

Having imposed her will, she displayed both extraordinary energy and willingness to accommodate different political views. When local disputes broke out in Castile, she would regularly arrive personally to establish a tribunal, debate the issues with the protagonists, and act as chief magistrate in imposing a solution. 'Exquisitely fearful' of baronial privilege, she was 'a disciplined and disciplining monarch' (183). Her energy was legendary: her reorganized royal council would meet regularly at 6am, and she continued to wrestle with administrative problems until virtually her dying day. During Castile's extended military conflicts with Moorish Granada, Portugal and France, Isabella assumed the role of military quartermaster to assure the necessary provisioning of the armies led by her husband Ferdinand.

Yet on one issue she was unwilling to compromise: the purity of the Catholic faith practised by her compatriots. Despite the acknowledged economic disruption and personal suffering stemming from her expulsion of the Jews, the forced conversion of Muslims and the persecution of *converso* Christians, she encouraged the Inquisition led by Torquemada and Cisneros to achieve the ascetic, pure Christian faith she personally espoused. Increasingly convinced that she was the chosen instrument of God, she could say to rebellious subjects of the city of Trujillo, 'I tell you that I will enter my city understanding that it is mine through God's service' (159). While able to accommodate compromise at the political level in, for example, allowing the conquered Moors in Granada to continue to live under their own laws, she was unable to allow a similar flexibility in the religious domain – to the point that even papal pressures would be applied – unsuccessfully – to adopt a more liberal stance. As her biographer writes, 'To allow [heresy] to continue, to deliberately avert her eyes from the crime was, to Isabella's scrupulous conscience, spiritually irresponsible, tantamount to committing heresy herself' (187).

The outcome of her 30 years of leadership was a more powerful and influential Castile – recognized in the marriage of Isabella's children with the ruling families of England, Portugal and the Habsburg monarchy – but one responsible for the terrors and dislocation of religious persecution. Civil strife followed her death in the absence of an agreed successor. Yet her will-power, energy and ability to accommodate different political views created the basis for the modern Spanish state, which a subsequent generation was able to bring under a single rule.

Case-Study: Leadership through the Marriage Bond

By far the great majority of the leaders profiled in this book made their mark on history either without a spouse or with one who played only a marginal or supportive role. Indeed one is tempted to conclude on the basis of this sample that extraordinary leadership may be incompatible with a balanced marital partnership!

Isabella was different. However single minded she was in her pursuit of Castile's unity and well-being, there was an important role for her husband Ferdinand. Although she was the dominant partner – at least as far as Castilian affairs were concerned – the two worked in tandem throughout their 35 years of married life without serious external signs of the friction which emerges in the conjugal affairs of so many strong leaders.

Their marriage itself was a milestone in her leadership. Having avoided one marriage forced on her at the age of 11 by her half-brother King Enrique and another by the death of her intended, she was well aware of the odds against her assuming the succession to Enrique. At 18 she defied Enrique to marry the heir to the Aragon throne, a splendid political marriage which would unite in one family the two neighbouring kingdoms as well as provide the military support she needed to assert her claims to the throne. Despite Enrique's naming of his daughter Juana as his heir, Isabella sustained her resolve until she and her husband had swung Castilian opinion in their favour as monarchs who would at last restore peace to the troubled country.

Their marriage contract established a political relationship which the couple maintained throughout their marriage. Isabella retained primacy in Castile, while Ferdinand would serve as her military defender and wage war on her behalf. He was to live with her in Castile but to have no sole powers there or even leave the country without her consent. While political circumstances in Castile dictated such a balance of power, the marriage was a successful one in personal terms as well: as her court historian Pulgar wrote 'the King's favorite was the Queen and the Queen's favorite the King' (89).

Their partnership was strengthened by their shared preference for resolving conflicts in person. Regularly Ferdinand would depart to do battle with domestic or foreign opponents while Isabella stayed behind to sort out conflicts at home. While she was prepared to accept his mistresses, Isabella was adamant about the appropriate political or military behaviour. Thus when Ferdinand's army retreated from an unsuccessful assault in Toro in Portugal and plundered Castile in its retreat, she greeted him with a lashing: 'if you had forced the forts open, and I don't doubt that you would if you had my will, Portugal and its sovereignty would have been lost in memory' (140).

The close collaboration continued during the exhausting war against the Moors in Granada. Typically, while Ferdinand led the Castilian army, Isabella would play an active role as quartermaster. Leaving the military strategy to Ferdinand, Isabella took responsibility for raising of troops and supplies. To quote her biographer ' not only was she a provisioner and quartermaster, but she had become a behind-the-scenes administrator and morale booster' (223). Even after major defeats such as Laja in 1482, she swallowed her disappointment and continued to support her husband's military primacy.

Arguably the principal leadership dispute between Isabella and Ferdinand took place in 1483, when Ferdinand decided to lead an Aragonese army against France to win the provinces of Roussillon and Cerdagne. Isabella, determined to continue the war against the Moors, disagreed sharply. In keeping with their joint motto '*Tanto Monta, Monta Tanto*' (one is equal to the other), however, they worked out a compromise. Ferdinand went north to Aragon supported by some Castilian troops, while his wife led the rest of the Castilian army southwards to Andalusia.

Isabella's determination, energy and commitment to the Castilian state have ensured her unquestioned leadership credentials. Yet her ability to work in tandem with Ferdinand despite these differences provided an extra – if not essential –

dimension to her achievement. Rare indeed is a partnership of sovereigns who for 35 years can reconcile their differences in favour of the interest of the country they rule.

Joan of Arc

Living the Vision

After almost 100 years of warfare against the English–Burgundian alliance, France in 1429 was dispirited, on the defensive militarily and badly led by the vacillating, insecure Dauphin Charles. In the brief two years between leaving home for Chinon and her death at the stake in Rouen, Joan of Arc provided a unique example of single-minded leadership driven by her vision of crowning Charles at Reims. She was truly 'the regeneration of the soul of a flagging France' (Sackville-West, 1936: 143).

Joan's leadership was her vision: a series of heavenly messages over a period of many years which provided detailed instructions on how to save the French monarchy, defeat the English and restore the French nation. As she fulfilled one prophecy after another in a string of military victories culminating in the battle of Patay, her following among the army and populace assumed a Messianic character in an epoch of superstition and credibility. In her words 'There is no help for the Kingdom but in me, since God wishes that I should do this' (84).

Her dominant leadership quality was a single-minded, totally dedicated pursuit of her vision. She impatiently ordered military commanders about – despite a frequent lack of clear authority – and fretted when Charles denied her freedom to pursue the enemy in Paris following his coronation at Reims. In hand-to-hand battles where leadership required close physical contact with her troops, Joan invariably thrust herself to the centre of the battle, urging her troops to a higher level of commitment. In the words of her historian, 'It was her single mindedness which enabled her to inspire disheartened men and bend reluctant princes to her will ... her courage and conviction were superhuman' (338).

With this dedicated pursuit of her vision, Joan blended her peasant's shrewd, simple and outspoken approach to both friend and enemy. A young farm girl with little formal education and no particular intellectual grasp of the complex world in which she found herself, she was still able to win support from hard-bitten and suspicious soldiers. She had 'no sense of hesitation, distress, shyness or embarrassment' (116) as she approached the disguised Dauphin in Chinon, dealt with recalcitrant captains, or defended herself against her judges at Rouen.

While her leadership role technically ended with her capture under the gates of Compiègne in 1430, her personal qualities throughout a full year of imprisonment contributed to the leadership mission Joan has evoked for generations of her compatriots. A girl of 19, without any companion or adviser and held in degrading captivity, managed for that year not only to keep faith with her vision but also respond with dignity, wisdom and shrewdness to constant questioning and mental pressure from a plethora of judges and accusers. 'Were I to see the fire, I would still say all that I have said, and would not do otherwise!' (292). Only at her final judgement, when confronted with her executioner, did she lose her courage and recant by acknowledging the primacy of the Church over that of her voices – only to reverse herself a few days later at the behest of these voices and thereby condemn herself as a relapsed heretic.

While other military leaders driven by religious visions – such as Oliver Cromwell – extended their leadership beyond the military sphere, Joan's leadership role was limited both by the nature of her vision and her own lack of experience. As the touchstone of her vision was restoring the legitimacy of Charles VII, she was helpless in the face of his own vacillation, personal weakness and gullibility. Faced with his own unwillingness or inability to lead, she could only resign herself to a role as courtier until requested to relieve Compiègne; and, when she was captured there, Charles provided the final blow by refusing to obtain her release.

Case-Study: The Battles on the Loire

Joan's leadership in the defence of Orléans and the subsequent battles on the Loire in the Spring of 1429 has come to symbolize the regeneration of a weary France. Without a formal role in the French military hierarchy or the clear support of the Dauphin, she set a personal example of military valour, single-minded purpose and religious devotion which was largely responsible for a psychological turning point in the Hundred Years War.

As escort to the French force sent to relieve the besieged city of Orléans, Joan first established her authority among her army by obliging them to go to confession and to send away their women camp-followers. Reluctantly allowing her escort to return to Blois without her, she proceeded in no uncertain terms to establish her authority over Dunois, the Bastard of Orléans who commanded the city's defence. Totally confident in the success of her mission to save Orléans as foretold in her visions, she brooked no opposition. On three occasions she confidently commanded the English to retire from their forts surrounding Orléans, an order which provoked an uncomplimentary response from the enemy.

After a week in Orléans during which she participated in some of the minor skirmishes, Joan joined an attack on the Tourelles, a fort held by the English in an island in the Loire opposite Orléans. As her voices had predicted, she was wounded; an English arrow penetrated her chest to a depth of six inches. Despite hard hand-to-hand fighting for 13 hours, the French attack was unsuccessful, and Dunois ordered retreat. Joan disagreed, rode off for a brief prayer, and returned despite her wound with her battle standard to lead the attack and eventual capture of the Tourelles. The seige of Orléans was lifted, and Joan's prophecy that morning of a victorious return to the city by evening was fulfilled.

The following day, a Sunday, Joan refused an English challenge to do battle, saying 'let them go, it is not the Lord's pleasure that we should fight them today; you will get them another time' (188). She thus held back the impatient French by the force of her personality, although arguably from a military standpoint battle should have been joined to take advantage of the English army's loss the previous day.

With Orléans saved, Joan could achieve her second goal of the Dauphin's coronation at Reims only by a compromise with the Dauphin which required capturing key Loire towns on the route to Reims. There followed a remarkable week during which Joan was at the centre of a series of French victories. A combination of the superstitious trust of the army in her predictions and her physical presence at the centre of battle overwhelmed the English defenders. 'In the eyes of the populace she was a leader to die for' (192). At Jargeau, Joan convinced the French captains to attack. When the English sallied out to fight, Joan threw herself into the mêlée, and the French troops, following her, carried the outskirts of the town. She taunted d'Alençon, the French commander, into attacking the town itself the next day. On a scaling ladder, Joan was struck with a stone which knocked her to the ground. She rose, crying 'Our Lord has condemned the English; they will be ours within the hour; be of good heart' (194). The town was taken. By now d'Alençon and the other captains, as well as the populace, believed that Joan was indeed sent by God to restore the Dauphin. Joan continued to urge the French forward, and her confidence was rewarded by victory at Patay. After the battle, however, she was found weeping for the souls of the English dead.

During these brief weeks, Joan's prophecies of victories were fulfilled by battles in which she led from the front. Soldiers and citizens alike came to believe in the supernatural dimension of her mission. Yet underpinning this mission was a single-minded, outspoken, unquestioning faith on her part which, coupled with her inspirational role on the battlefield, became a symbol of the French recovery.

Abraham Lincoln

Pursuing a Vision of Unity through Four Years of Civil War

Elected President by the votes of the anti-slavery faction, Abraham Lincoln on assuming office in 1860 faced the immediate secession of the Southern states and subsequently over four years of bloody, fratricidal civil war. The touchstone of his leadership throughout this period of agony was the vision of an indissoluble Union for which, rather than against slavery, his Northern armies fought.

Despite his personal aversion to slavery, Lincoln was aware of its divisiveness at the outset of the war as an issue for the great mass of Americans – as opposed to the concept of a united America with its enviable democratic tradition and economic potential. Throughout the war he confronted two articulate extremist views; the Copperhead peace party and the abolitionist faction headed by Sumner. His solution was compromise and conciliation: 'I pass my life preventing the storm from blowing down the tent ... I do not lead; I only follow.' (Sandberg, 1954: 345).

On the slavery issue, for example, he began the war by overriding local commanders such as Fremont, who authorized the freeing of slaves, and proposed negotiated, compensated emancipation deals. As the tide of opinion in the border states moved against slavery, he first proposed the Emancipation Proclamation for subsequent implementation and finally issued it in December 1862.

Another dimension of his policy was a total pragmatism and trust in his military and civil colleagues. Generals such as Grant and Cabinet ministers such as Seward, Stanton and Chase were trusted for what they did to implement his strategy – rather than heeding what their critics said about them or even their own criticisms of himself. Arguably Lincoln's greatest mistake was his sustained faith in George McClellan in 1861–2 despite growing evidence that the head of the Army of the Potomac was incapable of a serious assault on Lee's army. Lincoln was quoted as saying 'I will hold McCellan's horse if he will only bring us success' (111), and, referring subsequently to the criticism of Ulysses Grant for past misdemeanours, 'I can't spare this man – he fights'. Partisan attacks on Secretary of State Seward were resolved to Lincoln's satisfaction when he procured the resignations of Seward and another valued colleague – and happily rejected both. While his vision was clear, the objective clearly justified the means. 'I have never had a policy; I did what was best on each day.' (731)

But what carried Lincoln successfully through four years of frustration and sectarian conflict were the personal qualities of wisdom, humour, humility and openness which brought him close to the mass of Americans. By the end of the war in 1865, both friends and enemies acknowledged that Lincoln embodied the American spirit. He is likened to a wire cable by Harriet Beecher Stowe: 'He has listened to all, weighed the words of all, waited, observed, yielded here and there, but in the main kept one inflexible, honest purpose, and drawn the national ship through'. (470)

His openness was legendary. Several days a week he received in the White House any and all who wanted a word – or favour – with him; these were what he termed his 'public opinion baths'. His sense of humour was not only natural but came to be a necessary outlet for the frustrations of a war that stretched on and on. Threats of assassination, brutal criticism of the 'Gorilla President', the frequent opposition of his cabinet and party – all these he could shed without deviating from his mission, interfering with his generals' plans, losing his sense of balance, or showing a trace of vindictiveness or jealousy. When Washington was threatened by Southern armies at the beginning of the war, Lincoln calmly organized the resistance. When hawks called for war against Britain, he pointed out that 'one war at a time is enough'!

His signal leadership achievement was thus to bring to an end four years of bloody civil war – and to set the stage for a post-war period marked by compromise and understanding from both sides. 'Crafty, inconsistent, and dishonest when it suited his purpose … he never let his personal morality – which by anyone's standards was very high – interfere with his role as a political and military leader' (Syrett and Hogg, 1992: 108). Yet despite what Burns calls his 'colossal balancing act' (Burns: 391), his tragic assassination left the country without a similar guiding hand during the painful Reconstruction period.

Case-Study: Winning the Election of 1864

A pivotal test of Abraham Lincoln's wartime leadership was the presidential election of 1864, which was held after four years of bloody and inconclusive civil war. Lincoln's leadership strategy of building consensus around saving the Union had not been crowned with military victory, as a succession of his commanders in Virginia were regularly defeated by the Confederate leader Robert E. Lee.

As the presidential campaign opened in early 1864, he was thus pilloried from two extremes: peace advocates like

Vallandigham who were prepared to compromise on slavery to end the war, and abolitionists like Seward who pressed for more comprehensive action to free slaves. A nation tired of war was erupting in peace marches and draft dodgers fleeing the army; early in the year Lincoln suffered an outright defeat in Congress from his own party in attempting to broaden the recruitment base by eliminating the $300 payment for substitutes.

Cabals of leading Republicans, predicting defeat for Lincoln if he stood, suggested he step down in favour of a more popular candidate. Republican editors and politicians such as Whitelaw Reid, Horace Greeley, Simon Cameron and Thurlow Reed publicly stated that Lincoln could not be re-elected. The opposition Democratic party nominated General McClellan to bring together the disparate elements opposed to Lincoln.

Lincoln's leadership strategy for the election was, quite simply, to continue to articulate his core principles of primacy of the Union over any electoral consideration while at the same time making resources available for the military victory which was ultimately necessary to achieve that Union. Pressed to negotiate with the South without insisting on the abolition of slavery, he prepared such written instructions – and stuck them in a drawer where they remained. His judgement in choosing Ulysses Grant as his principal commander was confirmed when Grant rejected the blandishments of Democratic leaders and went on record as supporting the President. Lincoln refused to lift the military draft to curry favour before the election and openly criticized some of his Republican followers seeking lower draft quotas for their own electoral district.

At a personal nadir during the election year in August, Lincoln was quoted as stating 'I shall stay right here and do my duty; they may hang me but I shall never desert my post' (Sandberg: 586). When pressed to compromise his principles for electoral purposes, he would repeat his statement that he did not want the presidency at the cost of losing his country.

And his commitment to principle paid off. First at Atlanta and then in the Shenandoah Valley, the Union army was at last able to report decisive victories as Lincoln's patient support for Grant finally bore fruit. The leadership qualities of McClellan as a presidential opponent paled before Lincoln's steadfastness. Having been replaced as commanding general in 1862 by Lincoln for vacillation and lack of offensive spirit, McClellan proved no more successful than Lincoln in uniting the disparate elements who nominated him.

The final popular vote was a convincing 55/45 win for Lincoln over McClellan – a far cry from the conventional wisdom earlier in the campaign which consigned Lincoln to a one-term presidency. Military victory clearly contributed to Lincoln's majority, but in turn that victory was a product of Lincoln's patient and total support of Grant. Defeat in the election would have been an overwhelming personal blow as well as a threat to the unity he had tried so hard to create – yet Lincoln refused, even in the hour of greatest darkness, to compromise his fundamental vision.

Ignatius Loyola

Managing a Vision of Individual Salvation

Founder of the Jesuit order in the sixteenth century, Ignatius Loyola blended a passionate Christian belief in personal salvation with the ability to lead a truly global organization of individual 'Companions' committed to fulfilling this vision. His Society of Jesus was consecrated to saving souls through vows of poverty, service to the underprivileged and faith in the teachings of Jesus Christ. Following the sponsorship of his small band of brothers by Pope Paul III, Loyola became in effect the successful chief executive, or 'General', of thousands of Jesuits in Asia, Latin America, Africa and Europe engaged in propagating the Christian faith.

Loyola's disciplined, all-encompassing commitment to his vision is the central dimension of his leadership. Having devoted himself to a life of Christian service in his early thirties, he prepared his manual *Spiritual Exercises*, a guide to salvation which became the basic framework of the Jesuit order with thousands of new recruits 'making' the Exercises. Throughout his early period of teaching throughout Europe, he was regularly arrested by the Inquisition and other authorities concerned with his growing popularity – and equally regularly responded by a successful, vigorous defence of his beliefs. Having taken a vow of poverty, he continued to beg food and other essentials both for himself and others – despite physical weakness stemming from the self-inflicted trials of his period of penance. His commitment to share with others a personal vision of Christian service overcame threats of physical danger and inhospitable conditions: 'for 30 years I have never failed to carry out, at the time I planned, any matter of service for our God on account of rain or wind' (Caraman, 1990: 59).

Yet in his interpersonal relationships Loyola exercised this inner discipline in a liberal, flexible fashion based on trust in his colleagues and recognition of the individual personality of his dialogue partner. Even in dealing with Lutheran opponents in the fierce battle between Protestants and Catholics for Christian hearts and minds, his approach was centred on listening, a frank and open dialogue, and graciousness rather than a formal debate over the right way forward. Rather than simply caring for the spiritual needs of Roman prostitutes sheltering in the Jesuit sanctuary, he made real efforts when possible to re-establish them in their original family environment.

In managing the array of diverse personalities – including remarkable individuals such as Francis Xavier who joined his Society of Jesus – his biographer notes that 'he trusted all and left all free, restraining some, goading others, presenting to all the Exercises as a process of exploring the Godhead' (88). 'In a sophisticated society, he was always unaffectedly friendly, candid and direct ... what he said was simple but memorable, unoriginal but striking' (87). Eschewing a detailed rule book and strict bureaucratic controls over the thousands of Jesuits responsible to him as General, he relied on individual correspondence and a staff of one assistant to lead his overseas colleagues from Rome. A typical message in one of the 7000 letters which went out under his signature was 'I leave everything to your judgement and I shall consider best what you desire' (140). Having been unanimously elected Superior General of the Society because – in Xavier's words – 'he knew each of us best" (126) – he continued, with few exceptions, to match individuals with tasks successfully during the Society's early years.

And Loyola fully lived his Christian vision. Having spent his early career in self-imposed poverty caring for the poor and friendless, even as the leader of the powerful Jesuit order he continued to work with prostitutes and beggars, feeding refugees in his home in time of famine. He refused to permit his companions to be promoted to bishoprics, as inconsistent with the vows of poverty, humility and service. As a young preacher, he accepted no constraints on the free exercise of his teachings and was thus obliged to move from Alcala to Salamanca and eventually to Paris to carry on his work.

Following his death at the age of 66 in 1556, the Jesuit order continued to expand until, when Loyola was canonized in 1622, the Society had 14 000 members ranging from Goa to Brazil and Ethiopia. Problems of managing such a massive and complex enterprise – in particular candidate selection and training – were massive, but Loyola's spiritual principles and human values have endured throughout the subsequent history of this remarkable organization.

Case-Study: The Spiritual Management of a Global Mission

With the formal proclamation in 1540 by Pope Paul III of the Society of Jesus dedicated to representing the Pope and prop-agating the Christian faith globally, Ignatius Loyola embarked on a new phase of his spiritual life. Rather than leading a handful of disciples attracted by his personal values and deep religious faith, Loyola now became the chief – and sole – exec-utive of a global enterprise.

His leadership of this global mission was marked by the same personal warmth, concern for others and strong religious views as his early career as the head of a band of brothers. Renouncing a Rome-based bureaucracy which would have blocked personal communication, Loyola relied on written cor-respondence to provide guidance on every possible issue. Delegation of authority went hand-in-hand with this strategy; Loyola relied on trusted colleagues throughout the world to carry out the Church's mission. Written rules were only estab-lished on the instructions from the Holy See; otherwise the ideals of the *Spiritual Exercises* should prevail. Loyola's written guidance reflected his personal philosophy: as his biographer writes of a mission sent to Ireland: 'they were to be slow to speak, ready to listen for long periods; with persons of influence or position they were to win their affection, observing their dis-

position and adjusting themselves according to whether the
were glum, grave, serious, lively or lighthearted' (142).

Loyola's leadership style demanded the selection of truly su
perior representatives of the Society working under difficul
conditions abroad. A foothold was gained in Spain agains
considerable local opposition by Companions de Aroaz, d
Villanueva and Borgia. Rodriguez in Portugal and Canisius ir
Germany made good progress in establishing local colleges
Francis Xavier did the same in India.

Assisted by his secretary Juan de Polanco, Loyola personall
handled all the voluminous correspondence with the far-flung
Jesuits as well as the Catholic monarchs whose good will wa:
necessary for the Society's succcess. 'Our way of proceeding
provided guidance for the quarterly 'principal' letters whicl
established policy and could be shown outside the Society
Responding to overseas Jesuits who criticized the output from
headquarters in Rome, Loyola was firm but patient, pointing
out that 'as for your thinking that my letters are not wortl
spending your time reading, I have by God's grace time and t
spare, as well as the inclination, to read and re-read yours
(151).

Moderation and a trust in the individual characterize
Loyola's instruction to his colleagues. 'A kind confessor
broad-minded in his application of the principle of moral the
ology ... he was always counselling moderation' (153). In
dealing with those of other faiths, such as Spanish Muslims
and Calvinists, he focused on conversion of the individual, no
the renunciation of his views.

In setting out guidelines for Jesuits sent to Ethiopia, for
example, he recommended a liberal approach which acknowledged the unique traditions of the country. Over time Loyola
synthesized his thoughts in the written Constitutions, which established guidelines for the functioning of Jesuit communities
abroad. These guidelines were discussed in Rome with his
leading Companions and tested in the overseas Jesuit communities before being introduced.

Problems inevitably rose from Loyola's liberal management
of the Company. In Portugal, which represented roughly half,
or 240 Companions, of the total Jesuit community, the charismatic Simon Rodriguez deviated significantly from Loyola's
guidelines in his religious and management role. When trans-

erred by Loyola to Spain, Rodriguez returned to Lisbon against orders and was then recalled to Rome, where Loyola ensured that he would enjoy a comfortable retirement.

Following Loyola's death, his successors were obliged to put in place more solid structures and rigorous controls to manage the 14 000 Jesuits who were in place by 1622. Yet in the two decades during which he had built the Company from a handful of followers to a global organization, Loyola's energy had stamped it with his personal vision in the form of the Constitutions and the values of individualism and moderation which he held dear.

Florence Nightingale

Energy and Brainpower Support Humanitarian Values

Driven by deep-rooted humanitarian values, Florence Nightingale in the mid-nineteenth century achieved a remarkable range of reforms ranging from conditions in British military hospitals and standards for the nursing profession to a broader range of sanitation and other useful measures in India. She met entrenched resistance in the military establishment and government bureaucracy by a remarkable combination of energy, patience, charm and a powerful mind.

As her attention was drawn from one assault on human dignity to another, her values were refined to encompass support for a broadening range of action programmes. Nursing reform in London, battlefield hospitals in the Crimean War, sanitation in medical and other public facilities, and public welfare programmes throughout India were all underpinned by respect for the individual and his or her living conditions. She showed 'utter selflessness in serving and ministering ... [an] intense love for the race' (Woodham-Smith, 1950: 128).

During an active career spanning over four decades, in living to her values her biographer describes her as 'the rock to which everyone clung ... her calmness, her reserve, her power to take action raised her to the position of a goddess' (200).

As a lone woman with no formal political or other institu
tional support, she relied on a unique combination of leader
ship traits to deal with the inevitable opposition to reform: the
existing medical establishment, military commanders, senior
politicians and civilian and military bureaucrats in England
and India. Florence Nightingale's quiet patience and determi
nation were one dimension of her response to conflict and op
position. While constantly frustrated inwardly by perceived
failure, she demonstrated incredible fortitude and self control
to achieve her goals. Having studied hospital administration in
secret for eight years because of parental opposition, in her
first wartime challenge at Scutari in 1854–5 she insisted on
working within military regulations – despite their patent
inefficiencies – until she had gained the confidence of her
medical superiors. 'I have been shut out of hospitals into which
I had been ordered by the Commander-in-Chief, obliged to
stand outside the door in the snow until night, been refused
rations for as much as 10 days at a time ... and I have been as
good friends the day after with the officials who did these
things ... I have resolutely ignored these things for the sake of
the work' (485). Constantly frustrated in her efforts to gener
ate reform through government departments by change in
policies and people, she would nevertheless return to the
attack with renewed vigour and a fresh approach.

Her persistence was reinforced by a remarkable mind
capable of marshalling massive amounts of information and
shaping it into actionable policies bolstered by irrefutable evi
dence. While she never set foot in India, her expertise on the
subcontinent became a unique resource – 'a reference library
– to a host of British administrators. It began with detailed
questionnaires sent to every military post in India, progressed
to a 1000-page report on sanitary conditions written at the
government's request, and ultimately evoked the ultimate ac
colade from a newly-appointed Viceroy: 'you supply the
powder and I will fire the shot' (561).

Her persistence and brain-power supported another dimen
sion of her leadership profile: the ability to build close
personal relationships with decision-makers vital to the
achievement of her reform. Queen Victoria, prime ministers
such as Lord Palmerston, viceroys, senior officers of the War
Department and the India Office – all were the recipients of

her considerable charm – bolstered by her acknowledged expertise as well as skilful manipulation of the media and her other friends in high places. Her influence-management was well known: 'I have talked my way into the confidence of the medical men' (182). 'Now I perceive that I do all my business by intrigue' (119). Cogent argument was buttressed by the occasional document leaked to the press and a private word to a highly placed official.

Finally, an almost superhuman level of energy supplemented these leadership skills. Round-the-clock work under primitive conditions in the Crimea, various illnesses contracted during the war, and continued overwork led to her becoming a permanent invalid in 1857 – yet for forty years thereafter she continued to manage vast research projects, write lengthy reports, carry on extensive correspondence and meet a host of officials and colleagues while bedridden. In 1897, she reported 'I am soaked in work' (586). Like other workaholics, she drove her colleagues as much as she did herself, to the extent of pushing her close associate Lord Herbert Stanley to complete the restructuring of his government department until virtually the day he died.

Florence Nightingale's achievements are impressive – especially given her need in most cases to achieve results without the direct exercise of authority. She left behind professional standards for nurses through the Nightingale School, numerous commissions to investigate and implement reform policies, the eventual formation of an Army Medical School, new hospital and barrack designs and a host of legislation and administrative measures to improve the living conditions of both the military and civilians. Yet the absence of direct authority to implement reform inevitably diluted the impact of her leadership. 'Miss Nightingale's shrieks' were well known but often failed to mobilize the action needed to carry out the agreed reforms. As a perfectionist, she thus suffered; Cecil Woodham-Smith reports, "she must attain perfection or she had failed ... she refused to consider what *had* been done, and only what had not" (428)

Case-Study: The Crisis at Scutari
Introducing a nursing service in a British army hospital in Scutari near Istanbul during the critical winter of 1854–5 in the Crimean War was a leadership test for Florence

Nightingale which set the public stage for the rest of her career in public service.

At the unanimous request of the British Cabinet, she recruited and transported 38 nurses to Turkey in a maiden effort to introduce a professional nursing service in British military facilities. She was met by appalling shortages of all supplies, rudimentary facilities, and a wall of opposition from the resident British medical staff who shared the widespread view that nurses were ill-trained women of low morality. Nightingale's response was to work by the rules and only offer the nurses' services when requested by the medical staff. The stand-off was broken when a combination of a fierce winter and the flood of wounded from the battle of Balaclava forced the medical staff to call on the nurses, at which point Nightingale led her team to work by participating in a 24-hour daily battle to save lives. She was everywhere: comforting the dying, providing supplementary medicines from her own funds, and personally ensuring the cleaning of the filthy lavatories when the orderlies refused to do so. Her biographer describes her 'standing quietly and obstinately by the side of each [receptacle], sometimes for an hour at a time, never scolding or raising her voice, until the orderlies gave way and the tank was emptied' (175).

At the same time she had to deal with internal friction within the nursing team – Catholic sisters versus Protestants, upper-class women versus ill-educated working-class girls, and her own nurses against those who arrived under separate auspices. Her response was meritocracy: those who did not perform or broke the rules of behaviour were sent home, while those who were committed to the sick and wounded, regardless of background, were given more authority. Regularly confronting challenges to her own authority, she was successful in a formal investigation before the Hospitals Commission in forcing the resignation of Sister Elizabeth Wheeler who mounted a challenge to this authority. Imperfect compromises had to be negotiated to retain a rough balance between Catholic and Protestant nurses, and a running battle with other groups of nurses continued throughout her stay in Turkey.

As the flood of incoming sick and wounded mounted, the mortality toll from hospital-borne diseases like cholera rose until more British soldiers were dying of such illnesses in the barrack hospital in Scutari than from war wounds. When a winter hurricane struck, the bureaucracy-wracked hospital administration literally collapsed. Nightingale drew on her own funds to provide necessary supplies and effectively took over the running of the hospital. At the same time, she unleashed a flood of letters to England to win support both for resources and confirmation of her authority as the senior nursing administrator. Her ally the Secretary of War Sidney Herbert, as well as other ministers and influential friends, were bombarded with such requests, which produced results: Queen Victoria wrote a letter of support to the Cabinet in December 1854.

When the crisis reached its peak in January 1855 with 12 000 men in hospital – more than at the front in Sebastopol, Nightingale was effectively in charge of the hospital. In her biographer's view, 'Her calmness, her resource, her power to take action raised her to the position of a goddess' (200). Taking time from her work at the hospital and maintaining discipline among the nurses, she found energy at the height of the disaster to write a detailed plan for a centralized, efficient military hospital administration which, in September 1855, was adopted by the Cabinet when it formed the Medical Staff Corps. Popular fury – fanned at least in part by Nightingale's letters revealing the incompetence of the medical administration – produced a Sanitary Commission which confirmed her analysis and conclusions.

The arrival of spring and the reforms initiated by the Commission ended the crisis during which her leadership had flourished. She had combined a selfless, unceasing care for her patients which has become a symbol of the nursing profession, with the ability to exert stern discipline over her wayward and quarrelling nurses at the same time as she unleashed a most effective compaign to influence the military and political powers in London.

Pericles

Leadership by the First Citizen in Democratic Athens

During his three decades of effective power between 460 and 430BC, Pericles led Athens to the peak of its military, cultural and economic power and influence. His achievements of naval superiority, the building of the Parthenon and other architectural treasures, peace with rivals Persia and Sparta, and the maintenance of a highly profitable empire are even more impressive when viewed in the context of the virtually pure democracy he nurtured in Athens. Effectively all significant political, military and financial decisions were made by the majority of roughly 6000 citizens usually present and voting in public assembly. With most public officials selected by lot and virtually no standing army, bureaucracy or police force, a leader such as Pericles had to lead by personal influence – effectively a daily process of defending his policy verbally against all opposition, knowing that at any point he could be removed from office by judicial process, fined and ostracized by popular vote. His only elected post was that of one of 10 archons or generals, who were elected annually and could be re-elected as long as they won victories and maintained the confidence of the majority of the popular assembly. In the view of his contemporary Thucydides, Athens was 'in name a democracy, but really a government by the first citizen [Pericles]' (Kagan, 1991: 251)

The foundation for Pericles' leadership was his vision of a city-state made great by releasing, through the democratic process, the full energies and capabilities of all of its citizens. Having achieved effective power as leader of the democratic party against the aristocratically inclined Cimon, Pericles dedicated himself to making Athens in his words 'the education of Greece' and a city so beautiful that its citizens 'would become its lovers'. While rival cities like Sparta espoused an oligarchic or dictatorial structure, Pericles insisted that Athens' greatness would be a product of its democracy.

Such excellence in practice would be achieved by the wealth of Athens' empire; an impregnable military posture based on naval superiority and the walls surrounding Athens and its port, the architectural leadership achieved by the Parthenon and other gems constructed on the ruins left by the Persian armies, and the peace maintained with traditional rivals such as Persia and Sparta. In brief, as Kagan puts it, 'he saw the opportunity to create the greatest political community the world had ever known, one that would fulfill man's strongest and deepest passions – glory and immortality. Pericles believed they could be achieved by the citizens of a democracy based on legal and political equality' (137).

To achieve this vision in a democratic context, Pericles relied first on superior rhetoric. Acknowledged as the greatest debater of his time, Pericles stood up to continued assaults, on his policies as well as his personal life, in the popular forum of the Athenian assembly which brought the citizens together to debate the issues. Underpinning his rhetoric was a total honesty and candour: Pericles was relentless in forcing his peers to achnowledge all sides of an argument and draw the consequences of decisions taken, however unpopular it might make him. Under fire in 430BC following military defeat and a disastrous plague which decimated the Athenian population, he could still say to the Assembly 'if you were persuaded by me to go to war because you thought I had the qualities necessary for leadership at least moderately more than other men, it is not right that I should now be blamed for doing wrong' (241). He won that debate. Another element of his persuasive powers was to inculcate pride in their city and to demonstrate the necessary linkage betwen the city's achievements and the citizens' contribution to this success. Thus his much-quoted Funeral Oration emphasizes, like Lincoln's Gettysburg Address, the necessary contribution made by citizen soldiers who sacrifice themselves for their city.

Pericles was particularly adept in his ability, in Kagan's words , 'to formulate the democratic ideal clearly, to impress it on the minds of the Athenians, and to inspire them with the desire to achieve it' (151). It was one thing to appeal to their pride in the Parthenon and its surrounding structures; it was quite another to persuade them, as he did, to retreat from their Attic farms and houses and watch their destruction, from the safety of Pericles' walls, by Spartan armies.

A second dimension of his leadership was its consistency. Pericles applied a disciplined, rational approach to all dimensions of Athenian life. Although widely criticized by its subjects, the Athenian empire was deemed necessary by Pericles for the city's wealth and power. It would not be extended by force – especially if it disturbed peace treaties – but it would be defended firmly against revolt and non-payment of taxes. Clearly inferior on land to the Spartan military machine, Athens would surrender its land empire – even allowing enemy forces to approach the walls of Athens itself – in favour of a naval force with undoubted superiority in the Aegean Sea.

When the popular vote occasionally went against him – usually to send an expeditionary force which Pericles viewed as unnecessarily aggressive – Pericles would accept the decision without questioning the democratic process or losing his self-control. When his rational, middle-of-the-road strategy was under fire in 430BC from both hawks and doves in the Assembly, he refused to bend even through it was manifestly a failure in the face of an emotional, aroused Spartan reaction. Pericles' stubbornness thus may have become the model for Sophocles' tragic hero who refuses to change course once a policy has been established. As Pericles himself told the Assembly during the disastrous year 430BC, 'as for me, I am the same, and I do not give way; it is you who have changed' (254).

Finally, Pericles truly lived his vision in his personal conduct. In a world where excellence in battle was a measure of political leadership, Pericles during his career fought nine battles as an Athenian general and was cited for particular bravery at the crucial battle of Tanagra. Committed to beautifying Athens was well as building its wealth and power, he took personal charge of the building of the Parthenon and ensured that funds were forthcoming for his building projects by popular vote over a 15-year period. He lived simply, avoiding the excesses of many of his peers; when his consort Aspasia was personally attacked as a means of undermining his influence, he appeared in her defence with rare tears in his eyes.

Pericles' leadership ended with his politically-motivated trial and conviction for embezzlement. Although re-elected in 429BC as a general, he died shortly thereafter, having shouldered the popular blame for the plague and military defeat in a war he had advocated. Sparta subsequently defeated and occupied Athens, although democratic rule was subsequently restored in the image of Periclean democracy. In subsequent generations, Pericles' achievement has served to symbolize – by both advocates and critics – the virtues and defects of pure democracy. Pericles thus posthumously achieved his vision that future generations would acknowledge that 'we lived in a city that was the most ingenious and the greatest' (9). His epitaph could be expressed in one of his speeches to fellow Athenians: 'to be hated and unpopular for the time being has always been the fate of those who have undertaken to rule over others, but whoever aims at the greatest goals must accept the ill will and is right to do so. For hatred does not last long, but the brilliance of the present moment is also the glory of the future passed on in everlasting memory' (111).

Case-Study: Maintaining the Peace in an Unstable World

An integral dimension of Pericles' achievement was to maintain peace in the Aegean while he built Athens' economic, cultural and political power. In addition to a host of similar Greek city-states with whom wars had been fought in the past, Athens had to address the dual threats of Sparta – the dominant land power in Greece as head of the Peloponnesian League – and Persia as a potentially overwhelming military power on the horizon. The creation, and ultimate collapse, of the 30-year truce with Sparta is thus a critical case-study in Pericles' leadership.

Having determined that defending Athens' far-flung empire was central to his strategy, Pericles realized that peace with the traditional antagonist Sparta was essential. In one of the rare occasions when Pericles lost a vote in the Assembly, the Athenian general Tolmides led an army into Boeotia in 446BC and was decisively defeated. Bouyed by this defeat, Sparta invaded Attica and threatened Athens. In Pericles' view, the rational solution was to admit Athens' inability to maintain a land empire in Greece, trust to the strength of her naval superiority to sustain the empire abroad, and negotiate a lasting peace with Sparta. Such a treaty was finally concluded by Pericles in 446BC. The issue was whether peace could subsequently be maintained when both Sparta and Athens sought to maintain control and influence over their respective allies, who understandably sought to involve the other superpower's assistance in the inevitable disputes with their own dominant power.

Pericles determined he would walk the narrow, rational path between unnecessary provocation and firmness in maintaining order in his own empire. He sought first to establish pan-Hellenic bonds by sponsoring with other city-states the new colony of Thurii in Italy. When Samos, a member of the

Athenian empire, rebelled in 440BC, Pericles himself led the Athenian navy to put down the rebellion. His terms to the Samians were magnanimous, designed to forestall a repetition of the dispute.

A more serious challenge to the truce was posed by the appeal to Athens for help several years later of Corcyra, attacked by Corinth. Although neither antagonist was a close ally of the two superpowers, both Sparta and Athens were deeply concerned by the potential impact of this struggle on the balance of power. This issue was debated in the public assembly of Athens in 433BC before the envoys of the quarrelling parties. After much debate, Pericles persuaded the deeply split Athenians to take a middle course: provide symbolic naval support to Corcyra rather than engage in outright warfare or on the other hand risk the future loss of Corcyra's substantial fleet to an unfriendly power. The tactic failed as the Corinthians nevertheless attacked in full force and were repulsed only when additional Athenian support – sent despite the protests of Pericles – arrived to support the Corcyrans. A second Periclean measure was an effective economic blockade of neighboring Megara, an ancient enemy of Athens, designed to demonstrate the Athenians' determination to prevent the spread of the Corcyran war to Corinth's allies such as Megara. Finally, Athens took action against a colony of Corinth, Potidaea, to deter a rebellion in the Thracian portion of the Athenian Empire.

While each of the measures could arguably be justified as a rational middle course between aggression and pusillanimity, the net effect was disastrous for both Athens and Pericles. Athough King Archidamus of Sparta also supported a peaceful solution to the conflict, popular opinion in Sparta was sufficiently concerned over Athens' perceived aggression to break the truce, mobilize and eventually conquer Athens. Although the Spartans showed every willingness to negotiate, Pericles held firm to his strategy – even to the extent of refusing to lift the Megarian embargo as the only obstacle to a war Athens was likely to lose.

Thus Pericles' determination, his eloquence and his preference for a low risk, rational middle course first brought a welcome peace to Athens and subsequently unleashed a war which ultimately led to his own and Athens' defeat.

Peter the Great

Implementing a National Vision

Peter the Great's vision of a modern Russia, drawing fully on the best practice of Western Europe in the early eighteenth century, was sustained by an extraordinary level of energy, a pragmatic commitment to meritocracy and an iron will which did not tolerate opposition. In an age of autocrats, his personal vision became that of his country, and his long reign of 43 years permitted him to make some progress in bringing Russia into the Western mainstream. Conflict for Peter was largely self-created, in the form of a 21-year war with Sweden for hegemony in Northern Europe as well as his direct challenge to the traditional Russian culture.

With little formal education and a childhood marked by violence and conflict, Peter shaped his vision on a remarkable 18-month odyssey in 1697–8 throughout Western Europe during which he indulged his passion for carpentry and shipbuilding as well as absorbed the political and economic doctrines of liberal Europe. Creating St Petersburg from a captured swamp became the focus of his personal, political and military vision. He reshaped Russian bureaucracy along Western administrative lines, insisted on the importation of Western customs, struggled with endemic corruption, and built a military machine capable of holding its own with European rivals.

A corollary of this vision was almost perpetual warfare stemming primarily from Peter's view of an expanding, increasingly competitive Russia. His initiative in joining an alliance against Charles XII of Sweden not only absorbed at least half of Russia's GNP for over a decade but also almost ended in disaster; only Charles's rashness and an unexpected victory at Poltava in 1709 saved the day. Yet within a year Peter made the same mistake as Charles by attacking the Turkish empire deep in its own territory and finding himself at Pruth confronted with the choice between military disaster and a humiliating peace. As Robert Massie writes, 'The fruits of 20 years of arduous, colossal toil were about to evaporate in a day'. (Massie, 1980: 578).

Peter's vision was not shared by either the ruling classes or the great mass of the Russian people, but the Tsar simply imposed his overpowering will. Actual revolts by the Cossacks and Strelsy guards were brutally suppressed. In Peter's words, 'Moscow will be saved not by pity but by cruelty.' (266) Peter surrounded himself with competent lieutenants and companions who displayed total loyalty and generally owed their position entirely to Peter. Potential opposition from the Orthodox Church was addressed simply by not appointing a Patriarch on the death of the incumbent and converting the Church into a government department run by his appointed bureaucrats. Like his peer rulers such as Louis XIV, Peter assimilated his vision with that of his people; on the eve of Poltava, he exhorted his soldiers to 'fight not for Peter but for Tsardom, entrusted to Peter by his birth and by the people' (507).

Having been unable to shape his son Alexis into a suitable successor, Peter was so concerned about him becoming a focus for opposition that he acted as both prosecutor and judge in condemning Alexis to death for little more than articulating an alternative way forward. Consultation and consensus building were not part of his vision: senior political and religious officers were told of his intent to break with tradition by naming his wife Catherine as successor only on the evening before her coronation as Empress.

Peter's remarkable personal qualities were integral to achieving his vision. His towering energy was expressed in perpetual travels and inspection tours followed by a flurry of decrees and instructions. Conscious that he would have only a limited impact on such ingrained national traits as corruption and lethargy, he still used every ounce of effort and authority to initiate the process of change. In a metaphor acknowledging that a successful agricultural economy required water to be brought from a distance to a mill, he admitted: 'I am building the mill first and have only given orders for the canal to be begun, which will the better force my successors to bring water to the completed mill' (840). Unlike those of so many of his Russian predecessors and successors, his efforts were sustained by his pragmatism, openness to innovation, and, above all, commitment to meritocracy.

Thus one of his landmark measures was the 1722 Table of Ranks of the Russian Empire, which introduced the concept of meritocracy in government. Only in the case of his intimate confidant and lieutenant Menshikov, convicted on several occasions of corruption, did Peter compromise on this commitment. Peter was most comfortable leading from the front, whether working as a carpenter in a shipyard or leading his troops at Poltava and the Pruth.

Observing Peter on his stay in Paris, Saint Simon found him to be 'a monarch who compelled admiration for his extreme curiosity ... his intelligence ... he assumed majesty at its most regal ... at all times he was the master, brooking no delay and no opposition' (674). And as an orator at the celebration of victory in the Swedish war expressed it, 'by your leadership we have moved from non-existence to existence and have joined in the society of political peoples' (761). But in practice he could only begin the process of cultural change. And his will was itself an obstacle: his biographer Massie acknowledges, 'The looming, mercurial presence of the Tsar himself did not contribute to initiative and decisiveness on the part of his subordinates' (774).

Case-Study: Reforming the Russian State

Peter could ruthlessly put down revolts, build St Petersburg from the northern marshes, and defeat the impetuous Charles III at Poltava. But in the latter years of his reign he became increasingly aware of the need to reform the Russian state both to generate more wealth to support his ambitious plans and to be seen to improve the lot of his countrymen. He was well aware of the rampant corruption and inefficiency in his government – as well as its vulnerability to the autocratic powers of a ruler such as himself.

In an effort to develop a representative government which would function smoothly in his absence, Peter tried first the traditional council of boyars, or nobles. Finding this ineffective, he replaced them with a decentralized structure of eight provincial governments run by his senior lieutenants who theoretically could efficiently manage their regions and provide recruits and funds for his projects.

This too failed as his governors neglected their duties. Aware that he was part of the problem because of his insistence on absolute power, he established in 1711 a Senate with wide powers to act during his frequent absences. Yet he allowed his principal lieutenants to operate independently of the Senate, and he himself was highly critical of its effectiveness. The Senate's relative success was largely a function of the presence of Prince Dolgoruky, an octogenarian who was prepared to talk back to Peter. On one occasion Dolgoruky tore up a decree because he believed Peter had not reflected upon it; to a grim Peter he explained 'it is my zeal for your honor and the good of your subjects' (770).

Recognizing the inherent conflict between retaining supreme power and encouraging a competent executive body, Peter turned to reforming his government's administration. The concept of colleges, or functional departments, was imported from the West, along with foreign specialists deputed to advise their Russian superiors. Yet many department heads were ineffective, while open conflict existed between the Senate and the colleges.

Gradually Peter realized that he had to take executive responsibility himself. His efforts then focused on education and introducing meritocracy into the system. The concept of service by nobles was broadened to include the duty of becoming educated; in 1714 all young noblemen between 10 and 30 not in service were commanded to report for duty to the Senate.

Meritocracy was the basis on which Peter generally promoted men. In the view of his biographer, 'Nobleman or "pie seller", Russian, Swiss, Scot or German, Orthodox, Catholic, Protestant or Jew, the Tsar heaped titles, wealth, affection and responsibility on anyone who was willing and competent to serve' (778). In 1722 he embodied this fervent belief in meritocracy in the Table of Ranks of the Russian Empire. This reform, which remained the basis of class structure in Russia following Peter's death, established 14 ranks for each of three branches of state service. Promotion up the ranks could only take place on the basis of merit and length of service.

Yet corruption remained endemic in the state, which was widely regarded as a 'cow to be milked'. Peter's leadership produced few results – hence his weary complaint 'I can turn dice not badly with my chisel, but I can not turn mules with my cudgel' (782). He focused on corruption in the Treasury with a massive investigation in 1715 which revealed a combination of sheer avarice, bad management and confusion. To pursue miscreants, Peter introduced 'fiscals', or officials paid to track down offenders. Yet when the finger of guilt pointed to Peter's closest collaborator and arguably the worst offender, Menshikov, Peter refused to apply the same rigorous punishment meted out to lesser mortals such as Prince Gagarin, who was executed. Thus Peter acknowledged the limit of his meritocratic philosophy, componding a situation in which, to quote a contemporary, 'the Tsar pulls uphill alone with the strength of ten, but millions pull downhill' (789).

While Peter's leadership could thus be ruthless in establishing his authority and mobilizing resources for his favoured projects, he found it difficult to use his iron will and energy to enforce the meritocratic fairness needed to root out the corruption of the Russian state. Progress was made, but government reform was not one of Peter's most stellar achievements.

Albert Schweitzer

Reverence for Life in Equatorial Africa

In building and sustaining his hospital settlement in Equatorial Africa, Albert Schweitzer combined a high degree of moral leadership and the pragmatic skills of running a medical community under overwhelmingly adverse conditions, at the same time successfully appealing to a number of constituencies whose external support was essential to the success of the hospital.

Schweitzer's achievement over his life-span of over 90 years was exceptional. With funds he raised himself, he literally built in 1913 what became a 600-patient hospital in one of the world's most underprivileged and backward areas, handled its administration, raised its finances, attracted and managed a volunteer staff, and adapted medical science to the unique conditions of Equatorial Africa. His leadership talents extended from motivating his African staff and patients in what was often a soul-destroying mission to improve their lives, to captivating, at the other extreme, lecture audiences, publishers, wealthy donors, volunteers, bureaucrats and other constituencies whose support was vital for the hospital community at Lambarene.

At the core of Schweitzer's leadership was a deeply felt set of values summarized in his phrase 'reverence for life'. Having committed himself to a life of service and sacrifice by giving up a successful teaching and writing career in Alsace in favour of the deprived blacks of Africa, he coined the phrase 'reverence for life' in reflecting on the loss of values which he felt had led to World War I. Henceforward he consecrated himself to fostering the will to live in himself as well as others. His life was a totally transparent reflection of these values, as expressed by James Brabazon: 'he was to make his life his argument' (Brabazon, 1976: 160). When asked how he could justify his efforts against the massive problems of Africa, he replied: 'compared with the size of the task, the little you can do is no more than a drop of water in the midst of a torrent, but it gives your life its only true meaning and its value' (283). In living his values, 'I am simply a man who does what is natural. The natural thing, however, is loving kindness' (317).

Schweitzer pursued these values with a rare discipline and steadfastness of purpose. Having first determined in his early twenties that he would remain in the academic world until the age of 30, upon reaching that age he revealed to friends and family his unshakeable determination to learn medicine and consecrate his life to black Africa. After deliberately choosing a region – the future Gabon – which was one of the world's most underprivileged and deprived, he spent most of the remainder of his life in an environment of debilitating heat, grinding poverty and rampant disease, working for patients whose negligence, indifference, superstition and thievery would test the endurance of Job. Rather than return to Alsace for rest after the standard two-year African tour of duty, he was interned as a German national in 1917 by the French authorities and forced to return to a series of French internment camps which seriously impaired his health. Yet he persisted in the frustrating post-war period by launching what became a regular round of successful lectures, publications and fund-raising efforts for Lambarene.

The other side of the discipline coin was an impatience and frustration which was understandable given his energy level and the problems of helping his African patients to help themselves. In Brabazon's words, he was 'a tyrant to work with; indefatigable himself, he would work others to exhaustion' (324). Acknowledging his irritability when crossed in his efforts to instil in his African patients a sense of responsibility for themselves, Schweitzer acknowledged, 'I have always felt clearly that if I were to surrender my enthusiasm for the true and the serviceable ... I should be surrendering my very self. I am, therefore, as intolerable as ever.' (318) As an outlet for his anger in Lambarene, Schweitzer kept a store of sticks he could break when the level of frustration required physical expression. Tolerance in the hospital community was a precious commodity; 'day after day at least some of the Africans defeated him. They failed to turn up for medicine ... they consulted the witch doctor, they cut down fruit trees for firewood' (Brabazon: 346).

Perhaps the most singular dimension of his talent for leadership was an uncanny sensitivity for the motivation of the universe of people he encountered in his life's mission. Recognizing in his African patients a reluctance to commit themselves to a structured, Western-type effort to improve themselves by productive work, he pragmatically acknowledged to them, 'I am your brother, it is true, but your elder brother' (229). Prepared to berate them verbally – and occasionally physically – for such failures as thievery, laziness and lack of responsibility, he nevertheless achieved a pragmatic balance which earned their respect and even – as part of his disciplined approach – their contribution in some fashion to the upkeep and development of the hospital community in exchange for medical assistance. His anger was an honest expression of frustration, of 'tolerant hopelessness', which did not, in his view, undermine the key moral issue. As he put it 'The child of nature ... has only elementary standards of judgement, and he measures us by the most elementary of all, the moral standard. Where he finds goodness, justice and genuineness of character, real worth and dignity, he bows and acknowledges his master.' (230).

His ability to relate to a wide variety of European and American constituencies was even more impressive. In his biographer's words Schweitzer's 'concentration at every moment focused completely on whoever or whatever then occupied his mind ... sheer personal magnetism ... a combination of physical power, charm, dominating will, and quick responsiveness to everything around him' (15). Volunteers, government bureaucrats, lecture audiences, heads of French internment camps, wealthy donors – all were touched by his total honesty, sense of self-deprecating humour, and remarkable ability to reach out to them personally. For such individuals, he was 'the man without needs who was always at the disposal of the needs of others' (189). When combined with the trained oratory of the preacher that he was, the impact was overwhelming – in particular on an American public in the 1940s who saw him lionized as the 'greatest living human being' by popular magazines.

Finally, Schweitzer's single-minded pursuit of the success of his hospital community completed his leadership profile. As the decades stretched on, he in effort *became* the hospital. From the beginning he directed every dimension of its activities: Schweitzer 'was a headman in the village, a peasant on his farm, a superintendant in his hospital – all at the same time. He dispensed justice ... mended fences, dug drains ... at important operations he was always present, day or night' (339). Criticized for arbitrariness and unwillingness to change as he moved into his nineties, Schweitzer would lash out with a comment such as 'it's my hospital'. When friends commented on his modest tastes – such as wearing threadbare clothing and travelling third class – he responded by saying that 'Anything I spend on myself I can't spend on my Africans' (319).

The epilogue to Schweitzer's leadership following his death in 1965 is a multi-faceted one. The Lambarene hospital has continued under government ownership, even though Schweitzer was unable to put a successor in place. Perhaps most important is the symbol he has come to represent of selfless devotion to the underprivileged as well as the total transparency of his life. Schweitzer's example in the annals of Christian sacrifice has thus extended well beyond the award of a Nobel Peace Prize and cover stories in *Time* and *Life* magazines following World War II.

Case-Study: Building the New Hospital

Returning to Gabon in 1924 after over six years of enforced absence in Europe, Schweitzer soon decided that the original hospital site was too small. The number of live-in patients now exceeded 100, there was little room to grow food for the community, and an epidemic of dysentery made it difficult to avoid the spread of infection in the confined area. The resulting effort to build a totally new hospital – the present Lambarene site – is a case-study in Schweitzer's leadership profile of decisiveness, initiative and patience.

Having decided that a site several miles from the original hospital could be appropriate, he typically announced to his team, without prior discussion, his decision to transplant the entire community to the new location where it would be rebuilt from the raw jungle. He deferred his scheduled return to Europe to take charge of the year-long construction effort. Once again Schweitzer was a jack-of-all-trades: architect, financier, engineer, boss of the work gangs, gardener and chief carpenter.

His leadership of the African workmen blended infinite patience with energy and a sense of humour. Committed to the concept that his patients should provide some compensation for their hospital services in the form of a few days' work, he collected a team of more or less able bodied convalescents to journey to the work site. He wrote 'It is no easy task to embark them in the canoes for the plantation each morning. They prove, with every gesture of conviction, that their health requires that on this particular day they should rest at the hospital..... Some on account of wounds cannot walk. They pull at weeds, seated on the ground' (311). His powers of persuasion were enhanced by the ability to provide from his stores rations of scarce rice during the current famine conditions.

In addition to supervising all aspects of the land preparation and building construction, Schweitzer personally led the work teams each day. In his letters, he sets a typical day to music. 'A day with these people moves on like a symphony. *Lento:* They take very grumpily the axes and bush knives that I distribute to them on landing ... *Moderato:* axes and bush knives move in extremely moderate time, which the conductor tries in vain to quicken ... *Finale:* all are jolly now ... the wicked forest ... shall have a bad time of it ... If this finale lasts even a good half hour, the day has not been wasted' (312).

Schweitzer insisted on using local hardwood – despite the difficulty in working it – to extend the buildings' life: 'Any termite that tries to eat my hospital will have to see a doctor' (312). A garden was created with terraces well drained against the torrential rains. Schweitzer personally carried water daily to feed hundreds of fruit trees; aware that it was impossible to

stop the Africans from stealing fruit, his solution was to grow
so much fruit that stealing would no longer be a crime.

An argument with a newly arrived doctor from Alsace
ensued over the design of the main hospital building. In one
of the rare cases where Schweitzer reversed his initial medical
judgement, Dr Trensz persuaded Schweitzer to alter the
design and went on to identify the bacillus which had been
plaguing the camp and develop a vaccine against it.

In January 1927, the entire hospital community was moved
to the new site. Viewing their new facilities, which for example
boasted wooden floors instead of the earthen ones of the old
facility, the patients raised a universal cry of 'what a fine house
you've built us, doctor' (314).

In a land where there were few alternatives to personal leadership in achieving results, Schweitzer once again played all
the instruments in the orchestra: raising the funds, designing
the new community, leading the workers and establishing the
medical standards. In his final years critics attacked his domi-
neering will and resistance to change, yet one can argue that
Lambarene would not have existed were it not for this determined leadership in an extraordinarily difficult environment.

Josef Stalin

The Pursuit of Personal Power by the 'Master of Dosage'

While other leaders espouse a vision or values for the benefit
of their followers, Josef Stalin's leadership was driven purely by
an obsessive desire for personal power and control. As he outmanoeuvred his rivals for Lenin's succession, purged all con-
ceivable internal threats to his totalitarian control and drew
on Russian nationalism to repel the Nazi invasion in 1941,
Stalin gained in self-confidence and the ability to dominate
through a blend of terror and manipulation.

In a remarkable career in which he achieved the domination of a nation rivalling that of the Tsars and other totalitarian leaders of an earlier era, Stalin exhibited two dominant

skills: a single-minded, ruthless pursuit of power, and an out-standing ability to dissimulate and manipulate those he en-countered in his quest for this power.

Stalin's ruthlessness and toughness – reflected in his choice of *nom de guerre* (*Stalin* is steel in Russian) – evolved gradually during a career as professional revolutionary (including three testing years in Siberian exile), years of power struggle for Lenin's succession, and two decades of unquestioned rule during which repeated purges of the Communist Party, the army and the civil service ensured that no opposition to his hegemony would arise, whether from independent Kulak farmers, victorious generals like Zhukov, or popular leaders such as Kirov. As his paranoia and obsessive need for control grew, the ruthlessness of his purges increased, to make a mockery of the ideals articulated for the Russian nation by the Communist ideology he espoused. In the forced collectivization of Russian agriculture, for example, according to Alan Bullock Stalin 'saw no victims, only enemies to be beaten down, by what-ever degree of force was necessary' (Bullock, 1991: 323).

This single-minded ruthlessness was blended, however, with an instinctive feeling for the strengths and weaknesses of his rivals for power. Having won the respect of Lenin for his effect-ive management of the Party, in the battle for Lenin's succes-sion Stalin skilfully embraced the Bolshevik commitment to collective leadership in the 1920s while simultaneously gather-ing the reins of personal power through his dominance of the Party bureaucracy. Termed by his rival Bukharin as a 'master of dosage' of the poison needed to eliminate rivals, he was de-scribed by his biographer as 'a pragmatic politician, a master of intrigue, above all in the single-mindedness which drove him to devote all his working hours to thinking how best to manipulate situations and people' (205). Rivals continually underestimated him – in part because of his ability to dissimu-late but also because of his rivals' superior intellectual skills in the ideological struggle after Lenin's death. Having won power by intrigue, dissimulation and the ruthless exploitation of his Party role, in the Cold War years following World War II Stalin deftly maximized his negotiating position with the Allies over Eastern Europe but recognized the limits of Russia's power and Western determination in the cases of the Berlin airlift and the Korean War.

These skills, coupled with a mastery of detail, quickness of mind and capacity for hard work, permitted Stalin to die of natural causes in his seventies after more than two decades during which millions of Russians died from periodic purges attributable essentially to Stalin's obsessive determination to maintain absolute personal power. While this grim reality was masked by Communist dogma calling for the withering away of the state and the victory of the proletariat, for Stalin Russia's interests were his interests; even at the end of his life he would make no serious efforts to plan a succession which would continue his mission.

Stalin's defeat of Leon Trotsky for the succession to Lenin is one of the interesting case-studies in leadership conflict. While Trotsky through his successful wartime leadership and intellectual power could be regarded as Lenin's natural successor, in the confrontation with the determined Stalin he demonstrated a failure of will which ultimately decided the battle. At the decisive moment represented by Lenin's funeral, Trotsky failed to appear, saying later in his autobiography 'I knew only one urgent desire, to be left alone' (148).

Case-Study: Taking Power after Lenin's Death

Stalin's assumption of effective power in the 1920s is a classic case-study of a firm, ruthless leader overwhelming less determined and resourceful opposition.

During the turbulent period of the 1917 revolution and the civil war which followed, Stalin was a loyal follower of Lenin with no apparent wish or capability of assuming power. The dominant figure in the Russian Revolution used Stalin as a loyal administrator and trouble-shooter – an *apparatchik* who would sort out problems with his well-known toughness and attention to detail. Only when Lenin's health failed in 1922 did Stalin emerge as a potential successor, and then only in the shadow of Trotsky as the war hero and charismatic speech-maker. In Bullock's words, 'what marked Stalin out was his intuitive grasp of how administrative could be transmuted into political power' (125).

To insinuate himself as Lenin's successor required masterful dissimulation. One of Stalin's classic techniques was to be the last speaker in a debate – thus able to be seen to summarize the discussion but turn it to his own ends or appear to be playing the role of the moderator. In similar vein, he deliberately played a low-key role, on several occasions offering to resign his post in the interest of party harmony. In the critical months surrounding Lenin's death in early 1924, his rival Trotsky's apparent volatility contrasted sharply with Stalin's tenacity and strength of will.

In the Bolshevik party debate which followed Lenin's death, collective leadership was posited as the ideal, while the charge of factionalism was regularly aimed at one's opponent. In this context, Stalin's seeming modesty and silence belied his growing determination to win power. He was 'a master of dissimulation with a gift for political intrigue and manoeuvre which none of the other members of the Politburo could equal' (193). Playing a waiting game, he stayed on the sidelines until an opponent had put a foot wrong. As Bullock notes, 'he possessed to a high degree the gift of silence' (199).

As the internal debate raged on points of Marxist and Leninist theory, Stalin converted his weakness as a non-intellectual to a strength by playing the role of a down-to-earth Party organizer unskilled in Party rhetoric – yet able to shout down a rival who could be attacked as violating the code of collective decision-making. At the same time, rivals such as Trotsky came to underestimate the threat he posed to their own ambitions. Thus at the 15th Party Conference, ten years after the Revolution, Stalin successfully fought off an attack by Trotsky (who styled him 'the grave digger of the revolution') on the grounds of maintaining party unity, while at the same time challenging his opponents by offering to resign (only to be asked unanimously to stay on). Behind these public debates were Stalin's ceaseless efforts to place his own acolytes in positions of power in the Bolshlvik hierarchy so as to control the party machinery. While rivals expended their energy in debate, Stalin built his power-base in the Party bureaucracy. Thus, in the view of his colleague Ruth Fischer, he was able to present himself as 'a revolutionary who despised revolutionary rhetoric, the down-to-earth organizer whose quick decisions and modernized methods would solve the problems of a changed world' (Bullock: 214).

After Trotsky's exile in 1927, there were few challenges to Stalin's personal power. He then turned his attention to monumental achievements which would appeal to Russian pride and

reflect on his prowess as Lenin's successor – such as the collectivization of the Ukraine and the elimination of the Kulaks.

Like his contemporary Hitler, Stalin thus gained power by a
subtle combination of underplaying his ambitions, appealing
to the perceived needs of the power elite and tenaciously
clinging to the goal of undisputed authority.

Josip Broz Tito

A Determined Communist Shapes a New State

Josip Broz Tito's singular leadership achievement was to create
a Communist Yugoslavia forged in the turmoil of wartime invasion in 1941, the clash of regional loyalties, and ideological
conflict ranging from royalists to Stalinist Communists.
Committed from an early age to the ideal of world communism
as interpreted by Stalin, Tito moved from an effective under-
ground Communist organiser to the wartime Partisan leader
who, against all odds, defeated not only the invading German
armies but also rival Cetnik guerrillas and regional forces to
become the undisputed post-war head of a federal Yugoslavia.
He survived the trauma of ideological rejection and possible
invasion by Stalin in 1948, to create, at both the political and
economic levels, a uniquely pragmatic Titoist state.

The vision and values which underpinned this achievement
were those of world communism and its utopian goal of a
classless state providing a cornucopia of benefits to the
Yugoslav masses. From his early days as a Croatian industrial
worker in pre-World War I Yugoslavia, Tito was totally committed to the Communist Party and its vision of a better life for
the working masses. For Tito, the approach of World War II
represented a unique opportunity to translate this vision into
reality by overthrowing the royalist Yugoslav government,
which had outlawed the Communist Party, thus creating a
unified Communist state. In the words of his colleague and
biographer Milovan Djilas, Tito's vision was to 'lead Yugoslavia,
a backward and disunited country beset with dangers from

abroad ... to prosperity and independence (Djilas: 126). Although the break with Stalin in 1948 led him away from a slavish imitation of the Stalinist political and economic model, throughout his life Tito associated himself with Marxist/Leninist ideology and the supreme role of the Communist Party.

Tito pursued his goal of a better life for Yugoslavs through Communism with a singular self-discipline and energy. He had a 'burning sense of mission about his work, his whole life was committed, and if the worst came to the worst, it would have to be sacrificed' (Auty, 1970: 125). Decades of operating illegally under the royalist regime during the 1920s and 1930s included five years of imprisonment which involved, as seen by his biographer, 'periods of terrible self-discipline to avoid mental and spiritual demoralization. Broz was tough enough to stand up to it very well' (Auty: 70).

His determination in the pre-World War II years was tested as well by his masters in Moscow. Despite Stalinist purges in the 1930s which virtually wiped out the Yugoslav representation in the Moscow-based Comintern to which he reported, Tito would usually obey instructions to return to Moscow for an uncertain fate. As Secretary-General of the Yugoslav Communist Party at the time of the German invasion of his country in 1941, he unhesitatingly threw himself 'with demonic energy' (121) into the organization of a nation-wide Partisan military force which at the outset included only a few thousand guerrillas against several hundred thousand trained and well-equipped German troops. With his back to the wall in 1942, he nevertheless refused to compromise his leadership with Mihajlovic's royalist Cetnik force which was supported by the government in exile and the Allies. His determination was not even undermined by the refusal of his Soviet allies to provide aid until after the Allies had done so and the military tide turned in 1943. After more than three years of bloody reverses, desperate retreats and near-escapes, during which his German opponents termed the Partisan leadership 'as resilient as fiends' (182), Tito emerged as the undisputed leader of World War II's only Communist force to win national power through its own efforts.

A second fundamental quality of Tito's leadership was an intuitive sense of his followers' needs – usually described by his

contemporaries as his 'political' skills. Having helped shape
the Yugoslav Communist Party, he could relate particularly to
the needs of the typical Party member, who formed the core of
his political support. For Moscow, he was the ideal head of a
local Communist Party: obedient to the Comintern, effective
in his organizational efforts and tough-minded in disciplining
his cohorts. By the same token, an intuitive understanding of
his superiors' motivation probably contributed to his survival
in the turbulent period of Stalinist purges.

To his intimate collaborator and ultimate critic Djilas, Tito
was the consummate politician: 'Tito inspired fortitude and
energy in a manner that was fanatical, almost mystical. He
merged his personality with the Party, both the tangible Party
... and the abstract Party' (Djilas: 52). Another biographer describes his challenge: 'one had to be very political, to go deep
into a man's being to help him, to look at the good in him
instead of the bad, to encourage his positive characteristics, –
only in this way could cadres be built' (Auty: 64). By the war's
end Tito had emerged with a 'unique personal relationship
with the people as well as the army ... Tito's alliance with the
Party remained constant, specific, practical' – (Djilas: 57).'He
had become "stari" – the old man – a combination of father
figure, village elder, protector and legendary hero, and he
knew how to maintain the right mix of intimacy, aloofness and
authority' (Auty: 133).

Integral to this unique relationship was Tito's ability to communicate clearly and simply. In Djilas's words, 'he was clear
and simple even when he was attempting to conceal that he
was of two minds in certain matters. Everyone understood
what he wanted or what he did not want' (Djilas: 67).

After the war, his intuition was translated into a pragmatic
approach to political and economic issues. Not an intellectual
leader or innovator, he nevertheless sensed the weakness of
the Stalinist economic and political model as applied to
Yugoslavia. Moving with the view of his colleagues, he established a federalist state in which the country's fierce regional
loyalties could be managed. In the economic domain, he supported the evolution of workers' self-management and the
abolition of agricultural collectives at a time when other communist states stuck slavishly to the Soviet model which collapsed in the 1990s.

Despite the break between them in 1950s, Djilas summarises his leader as 'a politician of formidable resourcefulness, unerring instinct, and inexhaustible energy' (Djilas: 179). Another wartime collaborator, Fitzroy MacLean, felt that 'Tito brought ... leadership, courage, realism, ruthless determination and singleness of purpose, resourcefulness, adaptability and common sense' (Auty: 224). These talents were supplemented by another: a remarkable instinct for danger and an ability to respond effectively to crisis. Whether evading a German assault or manoeuvring in the Moscow political jungle, Tito was the consummate crisis manager. As he put it, 'life had taught me that the most dangerous thing at such critical moments [such as his expulsion from the Cominform in 1948] is not to take a stand, to hesitate ... reaction must always be bold and determined' (274). Criticized by Djilas for a host of military mistakes, Tito was acknowledged to be able to learn from these failures, being seen as having 'a strong sense of danger, as instinctive as it is rational; an unconquerable will to live, to survive, and to endure' (15).

Tito's leadership score was not all positive – at least as measured by the standard of the welfare of his constituency: many of his post-war economic strategies had to be reversed in the 1960s; a Stalinist view of political discipline produced the horrors of correction camps for Yugoslav communists who chose the Stalinist route after 1948; as his stature grew both at home and abroad after the war, he was widely criticized for vanity in his life-style.

Yet his leadership achievement is impressive – particularly in the context of the disintegration of the Yugoslav state following his death in 1980. While he can be criticized for not having put in place an effective succession, the inability of his predecessors between the two World Wars to weld together a durable state from the historically distinct Croat, Slovene, Serb, Bosnian and Montenegrin regions argues in favour of the view that only an outstanding leader such as Tito is capable of harnessing – at least temporarily – such centrifugal forces.

Case-Study: The Leadership Duel with Draza Mihajlovic
The wartime duel for Yugoslav leadership with Draza Mihajlovic provides a particularly fascinating demonstration of Tito's leadership talent.

Following the German invasion of Yugoslavia in April 1941, officers and men of the defeated Royalist Yugoslav army regrouped under the leadership of Mihajlovic, himself a Colonel in the Royalist army. Mihajlovic benefited not only from the legitimacy conferred by his ties with the former government, now operating from exile in London, but also substantial material and political support from the British government. His Cetnik (military company) force was resolutely opposed to Tito's tiny Partisan army; which as an avowedly communist unit was anathema to Mihajlovic's Royalist traditions. In Serbia, Cetniks and Partisans competed for support on the basis of their respective political allegiances. Eschewing military conflict with the occupying German army, Mihajlovic instead attacked Partisan forces and persuaded the British government to declare him Commander-in-Chief of Yugoslav forces in this struggle.

Faced with the problem of rival claimants to leadership among the Yugoslav resistance forces, the British government put heavy pressure on both Mihajlovic and Tito to negotiate some form of collaboration – presumably under the former's primacy.

Tito's leadership response was to negotiate, but without conceding this primacy. Even though Cetnik forces were attacking his Partisans and refusing to assist Partisan forces under German attack in Uzice, he met several times with Mihajlovic. An additional problem for Tito was Russian pressure not to oppose the wishes of their British allies. Tito thus offered a comprehensive 12-point programme based on joint operations of Cetniks and Partisans but with the latter retaining effective control. Tito even offered Mihajlovic the supreme command of this joint effort, although clearly retaining the ability to operate on his own. Predictably, Mihajlovic declined the offer in view of what he viewed as unbridgeable political differences between the two.

While Mihajlovic refused to attack German installations for fear of reprisals on civilians, Tito continued to amass popular support – despite bloody German reprisals – by mounting a nation-wide resistance effort. During the next critical months during which he successfully resisted attacks not only from the Germans and Cetniks but also the Croat Ustasi forces, Tito was able to prove to the British authorities not only that he was prepared to fight Germans but also that Mihajlovic was engaged in secret negotiations with the occupying German authorities. First Churchill and then Roosevelt were convinced by these efforts, and a growing flow of Allied aid in 1943 helped to swing the tide in Tito's favour.

Fighting the propaganda battle against the Cetniks at the same time as he was being hammered and pursued by vastly superior German forces demonstrated Tito's iron discipline and determination to achieve a communist revolution in Yugoslavia. A less committed leader could easily have compromised with either the legitimized Mihajlovic forces and their Allied sponsors, or even with the German occupiers. The disciplined Partisan forces – who shot their own troops for looting and insisted on carrying their own wounded rather than leave them to the Germans – eventually won the military conflict, and in 1946 Mihajlovic was captured, convicted of treason and executed.

George Washington

The Disciplined Patriot

As a soldier and statesman in the formative years of the American republic, George Washington provided leadership in a time of bitter conflict by embodying the basic values espoused by his countrymen: patriotism, honesty, integrity and the democratic process. With his total commitment to these values – as well as disciplined leadership on the battlefield against overwhelming odds – he was the universal choice to lead the colonies' army, head its Constitutional Convention, and win a remarkable unanimity of electoral votes on two occasions as the country's President. As Douglas Southall Freeman puts it, 'in nothing transcendent … he [became] a moral rallying point, the embodiment of the purpose, patience and determination necessary for the triumph of the revolutionary cause.' (Freeman, 1968, 264).

Perhaps the most remarkable dimension of Washington's leadership was his discipline – both internally and as a Commander-in-Chief. For six years until victory at Yorktown, he tirelessly dealt with shortages of all military supplies; incompetent and arrogant subordinates; the need to reconstitute his army each year from new recruits and raw militiamen; Congressmen and state officials who had to be cajoled into co-operation – all while combating superior, well-trained British forces with total command of the sea. Never losing his self-control or commitment even in the face of defeat, treachery, desertion or total lack of resources, he was able to rally his retreating troops at Monmouth Court House, ride for help after 12 hours of combat in the saddle after Braddock's defeat, and convert retreats into unexpected victories at Trenton and Princeton.

Enforcing discipline in an army understandably prone to mutiny and desertion, he was able to preserve an American armed force for six years until French reinforcements swung the balance at Yorktown. Adversity even appeared to stimulate him: 'The more nearly hopeless his task, the greater his ambition to discharge it; above all, he had the courage and will to go straight on where the road was blackest' (513).

This inner discipline and patient endurance were reinforced by his total commitment to a non-partisan, meritocratic treatment of his troops, officers and subordinates. Fully trusted by his men, he was able to avoid mutiny at the nadir of Valley Forge when 'our sick (are) naked, our well naked, our unfortunate men in captivity naked' (373). Arrogant and scheming generals such as Gates and Lee were praised for their military skills in a world where good American generalship was in short supply.

Accompanying this personal integrity was an equally total respect for civilian government and the democratic process. Responsible to the American Congress as Commander-in-Chief, he would take infinite pains to communicate openly with his civilian superiors – even to the extent of welcoming a series of Congressional investigations when he had more urgent military tasks to perform.

Finally, Washington was a true democrat in his commitment to build consensus through consultation. When confronted with a military issue, he would invariably call a council of his generals – and often follow the consensus even if it varied from his own judgement. In his relations with Congress, he would open his correspondence file to ensure that the legislators were fully conversant with the issues. As President, he would carefully solicit the views of his principal Cabinet members – often in writing – and generally follow the consensus view. His avowed objective was 'to learn from dispassionate men ... the genuine opinion they entertain of each article of the instrument ... my wishes are to have the favorable and unfavorable side of each article ... that I may see the bearing and tendency of each of them, and, ultimately, on which side the balance is to be found' (667).

In his striving for the right way forward, the national interest was his touchstone: 'my temper leads me to peace and harmony with all men, and it is particularly my wish to avoid any personal feuds with those who are embarked in the same great national interest with myself' (381).

On the other hand, his leadership skills did not include oratory, talent in debate or unique strategic insights on the battlefield. As the political debate during his second term polarized between Southern Republicans and Northern Federalists, he became increasingly frustrated and uncomfortable. Yet he held instinctively to his values of peace, the national interest and the democratic process as he piloted the infant state through the gathering war clouds of the 1790s. As Thomas Jefferson put it, 'North and South will hang together if they have you to hang on' (606). Washington's legacy of leadership through national values still marks the American political philosophy over 200 years after his death.

Case-Study: Valley Forge: The Turning-Point

George Washington's signal achievement for the American Revolution was keeping an organized military force in position against the British armies for six painful years. Arguably the nadir of this leadership test was the winter of 1777–8 at Valley Forge as well as the skirmish with the British general George Clinton which followed it.

When Washington's army encamped on the barren hillside at Valley Forge, he had already endured three years of battling inadequate military stores and supplies, feuding and disloyal Generals, a suspicious Congress, and an army which virtually had to be renewed and retrained each year – as well as fighting a superior British force.

The winter at Valley Forge, however, brought Washington and his army to the breaking point. Virtually no buildings for the army had been constructed when the fierce winter descended. Due to inadequate management by the Quartermaster General, supplies of food literally ran out in January, while inadequate supplies of blankets and uniforms meant that the army was half-naked, with men dying regularly of exposure. In addition, intrigue among Washington's generals reached a peak. General Thomas Conway persuaded Congress, over Washington's objections, to appoint him Inspector General with an ill-defined brief to evaluate Washington's performance. Despite Washington's constant but polite and measured pleas for support and resources, Congress and the State Governors met only a fraction of the army's needs. When asked by visiting Congressmen why he had not complained of the various cabals against him, Washington's response was, 'how could I exculpate myself without doing harm to the public cause?' (376). As an anxious Washington toured the Valley Forge camp in a bitterly cold January, he heard the ominous chant ' no pay, no clothes, no provisions, no rum' . Washington was fully prepared for either open mutiny or simply desertion *en masse.*

Yet neither happened. Faith in their Commander-in-Chief held the battered army together. Washington's patience, his calm but persistent and reasoned appeals to Congress for help, his ability to control his anger over the incompetence and disloyalty of key officers – all carried the Army – and the American Revolution – through another difficult winter. Washington simply would not abdicate his responsibilities, and his troops knew it. As the winter abated, the good news of the French entry into the conflict was received – the first glimmer of hope for ultimate success the Americans had received since declaring their independence.

But the saga of Valley Forge is not complete without the coda of the battle of Monmouth, which was fought in June 1778 as the British army retreated from Philadelphia. Moving out of the Valley Forge camp in pursuit, Washington charged General Charles Lee, one of his most effective but independent-minded generals, to attack the retreating British before they could reach the shelter of New York City. Instead, Lee himself retreated at Monmouth, and Washington, coming up in support, found himself faced with a disorganized mass of fleeing American troops with the British army 15 minutes

behind them in full pursuit. Washington's composure, resourcefulness and personal courage saved the day. Personally
appealing to the fleeing troops, directing their officers to
assume defensive positions and deploying his artillery,
Washington stopped the British advance and prepared a
counter-attack which was aborted only by the heat and his
men's exhaustion. By avoiding almost certain defeat at
Monmouth, Washington had once again demonstrated the
leadership which earned him the unanimous choice of Father
of his Country and its first President.

Woodrow Wilson

Pragmatism and Determination

Woodrow Wilson is a central figure in any study of leadership.
Rarely has a leader so effectively, and in so many career roles,
blended an idealistic vision with the necessary steadfast determination, pragmatism in dealing with conflicting interests,
and oratorical skills to influence mass opinion. As a progressive President of Princeton University, a reforming Governor
of New Jersey, and finally as wartime leader and leading negotiator of the peace after World War I, Wilson not only excelled
in articulating his visions but also committed all his remarkable energies to their implementation – which drove him to
physical collapse in 1919. Throughout his career he carried
with him his own vision of a leader: 'a great human being ...
with unflagging pathetic hope towards better things ...
[a man] big enough to think in the terms of what others than
himself are striving for ... he is a guide, a comrade, a mentor,
a servant, a friend of mankind' (Hecksher, 1991: 218).

As Wilson moved through his academic career into the political sphere, he evolved his liberal philosophy of social justice
and economic opportunity on both a national and an international scale. A unique dimension of his leadership was his
ability to elevate a policy issue 'to the ultimate level of principle – to convert controversy into a sacred cause' (199). His
own definition of leadership in an 1890 academic paper
equates it with high moral values: 'the motives which [leaders]

urge are elemental, the morality which they seek to enforce is large and obvious, the policy they emphasize purged of all subtlety ... men of strenuous minds and high ideals came forward ... as champions of a political or moral principle' (102). His achievements reflect this liberal commitment: a new curriculum at Princeton, legislation in New Jersey to reduce the role of bossism, national legislation on banking, antitrust and tariffs to reduce the power of the trusts, and finally the search in 1919 for a 'great peace, not a mean peace', to pave the way to a more liberal post-war world.

At the core of his leadership style was a thoughtful, intellectually rigorous analysis of issues. As a young professor, his lectures were meticulously prepared, while as a statesman he would take the time both to think out his position and to arm himself with its detailed defence. A journalist describes his approach to his legislative programme for the New Freedom in 1913–14: 'He is always prepared. He has thought out his premises and his conclusions. He makes those premises and draws those conclusions with pitiless regularity and cumulative force' (321).

The force of his vision was matched by his relentless pursuit and total commitment to its achievement. Criticized for armed intervention at Vera Cruz in Mexico in 1914, he acknowledged that 'we are expected to put the utmost energy of every power that we have into the service of our fellow man, never sparing ourselves, but ready, if need be, to go to the utter length of complete self-sacrifice' (329). The stroke which finally incapacitated Wilson in 1919 followed months of parallel negotiations with the European allies and Congress in which he alone bore the brunt of the exhausting negotiating process. Rather than delegate this key responsibility to his aides, Wilson in an unprecedented move for a US President spent months in Paris as the chief US negotiator to ensure that his vision was achieved.

While criticized for unwillingness to compromise his ideals, Wilson was nevertheless a skilled negotiator with an unerring sense of what was needed to achieve agreement from warring viewpoints. Whether introducing a new curriculum at Princeton with the support of the faculty, building consensus for a legislative programme, or negotiating in Paris with the Allied governments, Wilson achieved most of his objectives without vitiating their substance. In his battle for tariff legislation, for example, 'by merely standing fast, by never losing sight of the business for an hour, but keeping up all sorts of pressure *all the time,* [he] kept the mighty forces from being diverted or blocked at any point' (28). A French translator observed: 'this lay Pope, separated from everyone by an icy solitude, is attentive to the least movements of the crowd and obedient to its wishes as he perceives them' (446).

Wilson's verbal skills as an orator constituted an essential element of his ultimate weapon in persuasion – appeal to the mass of voters. Honed originally in the college classroom, where 'he had a contagious interest – his eyes flashed' (94), they were marked by lucidity, simplicity, a deep understanding of his audience and appeal to the emotions. Whatever his audience, Wilson could usually rely on his oratory to carry the day. His greatest failure, the inability to overcome Republican opposition to the League of Nations, occurred as he mounted a nation-wide whistle-stop speaking tour which might arguably have swung the vote in his favour had he not collapsed from a debilitating stroke.

Related to this oratorical power was a conviction that a leader's role is to seek out and identify the nation's true, often unarticulated, will. As a college president defining the role of a national leader he wrote 'if the President rightly interprets the national thought and boldly insists upon it, he is irresistible; and the country never feels the zest of action so much as when its President is of such insight and calibre' (163). The obvious risk is that the leader himself makes this determination. Yet in critical moments such as guiding the US through a period of neutrality ending in the declaration of war on Germany in 1917, he proved that he was in touch with strident as well as unarticulated voices.

For the student of leadership, Woodrow Wilson is of particular interest in demonstrating the limits of visionary or transcendental leadership. By elevating issues to the status of a vision to be realized, he raised the stakes in the inevitable debate with opposing forces. He thus met defeat after four brilliantly successful years as President of Princeton when he could not heal a split with the alumni over his efforts to restructure the college's residential system. In similar vein, having insisted on a peace in 1918 which would forestall

future conflict as well as settle the most recent one, he met
defeat in his efforts to craft a League of Nations acceptable to
the US Congress. Yet by articulating and espousing such a
vision, he created momentum which extended beyond his own
life-time – thus today's United Nations in many respects fulfils
the vision Wilson outlined for his League of Nations.

Case-Study: Enacting the New Freedom Legislation

Woodrow Wilson's mastery of political leadership is arguably
best demonstrated by his successful sponsorship of reform
legislation following election as President in 1912. Building on
his success as a reform Governor of New Jersey, he structured
his legislative programme around the reform of the tariff (the
Underwood Tariff), banking regulation (the Federal Reserve
Act), and restraint of trade (the Clayton Act). As in his earlier
leadership achievements, Wilson in his 1913 New Freedom
legislative programme successfully blended a deep understanding of the electorate's needs, steady commitment to his
long-term objective, firm and bold management of the legislative progress, patience, and a deft manipulation of key legislative figures to achieve his goals.

Thus tariff liberalization, designed to break the power of
the trusts, was the first priority. His innate sense of the popular
will recognized the electoral mandate for breaking the power
of entrenched interests. Faced with the failure of his predecessors to overcome regional protectionist interests, Wilson
seized the initiative with an unprecedented direct address to
Congress and a well-publicized unwillingness to compromise
on such key elements as tariff-free wool and sugar. He used
loyal Democratic Congressmen, such as Oscar Underwood, to
overcome the inevitable parochial interests. A horde of lobby-
ists who descended on Washington were undermined and dis-
credited by Wilson's encouragement of a public investigation
into their motives and techniques. As Senate debate threatened to rumble on throughout the summer, Wilson reinforced his public determination with the decision to stay in
Washington to fight daily for his legislation at the expense of
all other commitments.

The companion legislation to create the Federal Reserve
was aimed at providing a liberalized credit system to comple-
ment trade liberalization. Wilson took the bold step of

running the two proposals through Congress concurrently, convinced that popular support would create pressure on Congress to approve both measures – a unique legislative feat for a special session. On this more complex subject he faced greater bipartisan Congressional opposition as well as the massed ranks of unhappy bankers. In this instance he chose the role of 'detached but powerful party chief' (Hecksher, 1991: 317) and was prepared to be flexible on the vital issue of public versus private sector control of the Federal Reserve System. Midway through the legislative process, Wilson shifted his position under pressure from his progressive supporters to favour effective government control of the Federal Reserve Board. Wilson patiently guided a split Democratic party through to passage in the House. In the Senate, where he was opposed by three powerful Democrats on the Banking Committee, Wilson swallowed his anger, courted the renegade Senators at the White House, and finally broke the bill loose from committee for a positive Senate vote.

In a matter of months, the new President had won unprecedented victories for reform. Subsequent legislation included the Clayton Act to liberalize competitive practices, but the approaching war obliged Wilson to turn his hand to the international domain in which he was a relative neophyte. At the apogee of his domestic reform programme in 1913, however, he was lauded by partisans and opponents alike as a master of the legislative process. The quality of his preparedness, even on complex issues, his patience and tact, his sense of the public will, and above all his steadfast determination to achieve his objective characterized this apogee of his legislative success.

Shigeru Yoshida

One Man's Values Shape Post-war Japan

Having retired at the age of 60 from an unremarkable diplomatic career in 1938, Shigeru Yoshida during an eight-year leadership period following World War II shaped the economic, political and social framework of post-war Japan from the chaos and despair of a defeated nation. Nicknamed 'one man' for his strongly held views, Yoshida during the 'Yoshida Era' was able to blend the conservative values of pre-war Meiji Japan with the framework imposed by the victorious American authorities to forge a national consensus which has endured for the four decades following his fall from power in 1954.

Yoshida's ingrained personal values underpinned his leadership success. Raised in the Meiji tradition of loyalty to the Emperor, conservatism in political and economic thought and belief in Japan's imperial role in Asia, Yoshida early in his diplomatic career grafted on to these generational values his personal belief that they could only be realized in close alliance with a major Western power such as the United States or Great Britain. As Ambassador to London in the late 1930s, he unsuccessfully strove to avoid war through such a pact with Great Britain and was thus one of the few 'fishers for peace' among the Japanese political establishment regarded by the United States occupational authorities as eligible for political leadership in 1945. Thus resurrected by chance from retirement, Yoshida proceeded in the 1946–54 'Yoshida Era' to establish his own leadership credentials. To quote his biographer, 'his postwar regenesis ... involved no ... sacrifice of basic values and priorities ... he had staked out his terrain long before and sought to win the peace on his own grounds.' (Dower, 1988: 274).

'One man' was a nickname well earned in Yoshida's persistent, determined pursuit of these traditional and personal values. As a diplomat in China and Europe, he was outspoken in criticizing his government's increasingly aggressive China policy, although his own vision of Japan playing an imperial role there akin to Britain in India and Egypt might well have produced the same end result. As war clouds gathered, he struggled to find common ground between Tokyo, London and Washington, even to the extent of losing his credibility among Western diplomats for unrealistic and wishful thinking as the Japanese military drove the country towards war. During World War II, he was the centre of the Yoshinsen group of traditionalists which openly advocated a negotiated peace, with a brief jail term in 1945 which firmly established his credentials as a 'fisher for peace' . Thus, after the surrender a few months later, 'his confidence ... was only rarely shattered ... it stayed him against the initial shock and despair suffered by many of his countrymen ... [it] enabled him to hold steadily to a conservative and non-reformist position ... and it provided for some Japanese citizens a small, tough, cantankerous personal symbol of hope and confidence in Japan and the future.' (194). As he states in his memoirs, 'I can be seen as a person who does not yield to coercion by others, but rather opposes such coercion to the breaking point.' (20).

The other essential dimension of his leadership was an ability to balance conflicting interests in pursuit of his values. As Japanese Consul General in Mukden (Manchuria) in the 1920s, Yoshida had to reconcile his government's offical Chinese policy, an increasingly aggressive Japanese military and various Chinese political factions, as well as the interests of the various Western powers. In 1946, faced as Prime Minister with a US occupation policy committed to uprooting the traditional Meiji institutions and values to which he and most of his countrymen were personally committed, he successfully resisted some US directives (such as those on political and economic decentralization) while espousing others (such as relegation of the Emperor to a figurehead role, and agrarian reform). His mastery of political subterfuge was fully tested in the early 1950s when US policy insisted on a massive remilitarization of Japan in direct contradiction to the constitution they had imposed a few years previously. His 'curious combination of decisiveness and ambiguity' (399) in 'adapting democracy to local conditions' enabled him for eight years to balance US pressure with an electorate increasingly concerned with its national interests and identity. He was 'bouncing like a ball in a game dominated by conservative players in both Washington and Tokyo' (418). By 1954, Yoshida in his efforts to reconcile these national interests 'was virtually a one-man show: now the sword swallower, now the contortionist, now the Houdini who made elephants appear and disappear' (439).

Yashida's leadership period ended in 1954 when the political left and right united to oust him as Liberal Party leader in favour of a replacement presumed more likely to assert Japanese interests in the dialogue with the US. Yet the Yoshida era laid the groundwork for a Japanese political framework which endures four decades later: a tripartite alliance of business, bureaucrats and politicians dedicated to a conservative ideology. His successors have included protégés such as Ikeda Hayato and Sato Eisaku who have sustained the tradition, and the issues of economic and political links with the US continue to dominate the Japanese political scene in the 1990s.

Case-Study: The Skilful Intermediary

Yoshida's skilful balancing of Japanese and American objectives from 1949 to 1954 is a fascinating case-study in political leadership.

The American occupation forces under General MacArthur were initially determined to restructure Japanese society: remove the Emperor from a political role; create democracy through decentralization of power; break down the concentration of economic power represented by the *zaibatsu* groups and eliminate militarism. When the Korean war began, the Americans insisted on using Japanese resources to sustain their forces in Korea. In contrast, the majority of the Japanese people desired some continuing role for the Emperor and no involvement in military conflicts generated by American foreign policy. Breaking down big business met serious resistance, while the American cry for grass-roots democracy found little positive echo. Appearing to kowtow to the American occupiers was guaranteed to lose votes in the new democratically elected Diet, while resisting American demands could lead to their imposition over his head by the all-powerful occupying forces.

For five crucial years, Yoshida successfully balanced these opposing forces. His pro-American and democratic wartime and pre-war credentials sustained his credibility with the occupation forces, while his ability to win on matters of substance buoyed his party in the Diet.

Thus Yoshida quietly espoused the fundamental American demands for demilitarization, a political alliance with the US, and the introduction of democratic reforms and civil liberties through a new constitution. On the sensitive issue of the Emperor's role, he conceded the loss of titular political and military authority rather than have it imposed upon his government. Yoshida also reluctantly but pragmatically accepted land reform, which ultimately generated the backbone of support for his party.

On the other hand, he successfully resisted the decentralization of government power as well as the break up of the *zaibatsu*. While accepting local autonomy in principle, in practice he vitiated the US occupational strategy by not committing sufficient resources to its implementation. The decentralization of police, education and other functions was thus eventually reversed. In sum, with the Americans he played the role of a good loser – but one prepared to reverse policies once the victor had left the scene. After his retirement he wrote: 'whatever harm was done through the occupation forces not listening to what I had to say could be remedied after we had regained our independence' (312).

Yoshida skilfully used the left-wing opposition, built around the vocal labour unions, to achieve his objectives. While the opposition attacked him as a capitalist tool, he could reinforce his credentials with American authorities concerned with the post-war Communist threat. Yoshida's savage attacks on the left-wing parties thus gained the support of the Occupation, delighted to find a real cold warrior and defender of traditional values in the Japanese Prime Minister. As for the conservative forces which had dominated pre-war Japan with the military – the major corporations and the government bureaucracy – Yoshida was able to forge a tripartite alliance which has lasted into the 1990s.

Yet his alignment with America, incorporated in the peace settlement he negotiated in 1951, was far from popular in Japan. Only 41 per cent of a poll sample had a positive impression of the settlement, and his popularity rating sank to 20 per cent as debate was engaged in the Diet.

Both privately and publicly Yoshida argued that the only means of ending the Occupation and restoring the national identity was to maintain the US alliance. Ambiguity was particularly necessary in the debate over rearmament. Widespread neutralist sentiment in Japan resisted any form of military capability, while the American government, confronted with possible defeat in Korea from superior Chinese forces, was demanding vigorous measures to support their effort in Korea.

With the peace settlement in 1951 and lifting of the Occupation in 1952, Yoshida had effectively launched post-war Japan on a course consistent with his view of the country's fundamental values and objectives. His post-war leadership thus blended his commitment to basic values with a delicate sense of the possible. In 1954, he reached the limit of his ability to balance American and Japanese views on rearmament and support of the American military presence in Korea. Japanese concern with 'war-loving America' and the subordination of her economic interests to American objectives were what ultimately threw him from office – but these conflicts have continued to preoccupy the two governments ever since.

Part II
Findings and Conclusions

1 Direction: The Role of Vision and Values

Contemporary literature on leadership emphasizes the central role of a shared vision among the group to be led (Kouzes and Posner; Bennis; Bass). Such a vision sets a challenging but achievable goal which is presumed to appeal to the common aspirations and values of the relevant audience. The leader's tasks are to articulate the vision, convince his followers that it merits their commitment, and lead them in executing it.

In the business world, to which most of the literature is devoted, the vision usually relates to superior achievement: leadership in a specific market, excelling in key performance dimensions such as innovation or service quality, or achieving a challenging financial target. In the military domain, it can represent conquest, successful defence of the nation, or the capability of achieving these ends by building the appropriate military machine. In the political world, such a vision might relate to achieving and maintaining values such as political independence, liberal democracy, a federal state or a standard of economic wealth.

Behind such a vision, however, usually lie such values as toleration, honesty, meritocracy and innovation. Often a vision is defined in terms of achieving and living these values. To a great extent, vision and values are thus inextricably combined. Such transcendental leadership 'seeks to satisfy higher needs and engage the full person of the follower', according to the widely used distinction established by Burns (1978: 4).

The initial finding of this book is that direction, rather than a specific vision or values, is the common denominator of the leadership universe portrayed. Throughout their leadership careers, each of the 25 has made a total commitment to move their relevant community in a single direction. That direction might be expressed in terms of a well-articulated vision, but equally well in a set of firmly held values. One of these values might simply be personal power, to which goal all the leaders' energies are committed, usually well screened by a publicly-

articulated set of national values or vision. The values themselves – such as personal religious salvation, democracy, national independence, tolerance or personal sacrifice – are
often elevated by the leader to the status of an all-encompassing vision or transcendental leadership.

In contrast to the current emphasis in business literature on
a vision for the relevant community or constituency, the great
majority of the leaders under review were driven by deeply felt
personal values – including the commitment to power. Only a
few, such as Ataturk, Hitler, Joan of Arc and Pericles, actually
elaborated a vision of a future community they were committed to implement.

Whatever the mix of values and vision, these leaders provide
direction. The compass needle of their leadership never
wavers: only death, physical disability or forcible removal from
the political scene terminates their efforts. Invariably the direction is a simple, straightforward one which can be expressed in a few words: a Christian nation (Isabella of Castile),
reverence for life (Schweitzer), truth through sacrifice
(Gandhi), human dignity (Florence Nightingale) or national
resurrection (Hitler). The direction is constantly repeated and
emphasized by the leader's words and actions.

The analogy of a compass-bearing was also used by an
American college president: 'the angle into the wind is less important than choosing one and sticking reasonably to it'
(Bennis and Nanus: 44). In some cases the direction is
modified as the leader gains power, becomes aware of his potential, and seeks to impose his will on a larger community.
Thus Napoleon, de Gaulle and Stalin become more ambitious
in their desire to expand their power-base. Yet their ambition
drove them roughly in the same direction.

In a time of conflict, these simple, powerful messages
provide a battle-cry uniting followers. In a polarized environment such as a civil war or struggle to create a new economic,
moral or political entity, potential followers can disagree with
the leader's direction, but there is no mistaking what it is.
Opponents who are seen to vacillate lose their claim to leadership; some of these examples will be discussed below in contrast to the leaders examined in Part I. As Gardner explains, 'a
leader who is unpredictable poses a nerve-wracking problem
for followers' (1990: 32).

Most important of all, however, is the bond of trust created by a predictable message. Bennis points out that 'trust is the emotional glue that binds followers and leaders together' (1989: 153). 'The truth is that we trust people who are predictable, whose positions are known and who keep at it' (44).

Yet the leader might have to provide direction for years, if not decades, to achieve the vision or values articulated. Even though his direction is clear, the call from the followership may not come until well after normal retirement age, as in the case of Shigeru Yoshida and Winston Churchill. Perhaps the most powerful message of these case-studies is the strength of the forces against which the individual leader must struggle. Even in the presence of such powerful leaders as Abraham Lincoln, Henri IV of France and Isabella of Castile, civil strife continues for years before the goal of domestic peace is achieved. Able leaders like Oliver Cromwell, Joan of Arc and Mohandas Gandhi can struggle for years to achieve their vision, yet their achievements may crumble after their death or departure from the scene. Pericles and Napoleon dominated their communities for years but were eventually ousted by the forces they had previously mastered. And strong leaders like Hitler, Josef Stalin and Charles de Gaulle may sit on the sidelines for years before being able to exercise their leadership.

The mix of vision and values incorporated in the direction shown by these leaders varies widely. A host of cultural, circumstantial and stylistic variables understandably play an important role. Above all, however, is discipline. As Kouzes and Posner put it, 'leadership is disciplined passion'. (xvii)

At one extreme are those leaders whose well-articulated visions fit the paradigm of much of today's current leadership literature. **Joan of Arc** burst upon the French political scene during the Hundred Years War with a detailed vision of a monarch restored and a France rescued from a debilitating war with the Burgundians and the English. Against all odds, she personally led the French armies to victories which enabled her to ensure the crowning of Charles VII at Reims. **Adolf Hitler's** *Mein Kampf*, written a decade before he emerged from obscurity to assume power in 1933, articulated a detailed programme of German national renewal and fulfilment – the Thousand Year Reich – to which Hitler com-

mitted himself totally until his suicide in Berlin in the closing
days of the war he had provoked to achieve that vision.

At the other end of the political spectrum is **Pericles**, whose
vision of the Athenian community elevated by democracy out-
lasted his defeat by these same democratic forces. **Tito's** leadership was driven by the vision of an independent, unified
Yugoslavia in which the communist party would provide both
material and ideological benefits.

Several political leaders conceived a remodelling and re-
shaping of a national entity along Western lines. **Kemal
Ataturk** thus shaped modern Turkey from the ashes of defeat
in World War I into a secular, broadly based and constitutional
state against fierce internal and external opposition. **Peter the
Great** in like fashion followed a Western model to create
a powerful state capable of playing a major role on the
eighteenth-century European chessboard. His iron will in eliminating opposition and allocating massive resources to the new
Russia typified the total commitment of these leaders to the direction they have chosen for their nation state. **Charles de
Gaulle's** rigid vision of a great France with himself as the
arbiter of her interests is a more recent example of the same
iron determination which will accept no compromise. **Shigeru
Yoshida** in post-war Japan was able to blend his personal commitment to a Western alliance with traditional Meiji values to
create a state whose political structure still endures.

Another category of leader represented by our universe is
the builder or conqueror. These may have a specific vision of
their own, but more frequently their personal drive for power
and influence – thus defining their followers' interest in terms
of their own personal objectives – simply drives them in their
chosen direction as far as the opposing forces will allow. Quite
frequently, the leader's direction is defined solely in terms of
his or her own ambition – albeit clothed for external con-
sumption in some form of national or organizational vision
and values.

A classic conqueror in these terms is **Alexander the Great**,
who set for himself the goal of becoming 'King of All Asia'. In
a decade of conquest during which he marched his
Macedonian army 17 000 miles to the Himalayas, he was
guided essentially by the goal of personal power and glory. On
his deathbed with no succession to his remarkable empire

planned, he appeared to have no regret over the inevitable debilitating struggle for power about to take place among his generals.

Napoleon's decade of conquest began as a defensive effort to save the French Revolution, evolved into a vehicle to free others from their traditional rulers, and ended as an empire so powerful that it set in motion opposing forces to bring it down in ruins. In similar vein, **Bolivar** aped his role model Napoleon by anticipating a vision of a continent freed from Spanish tyranny. Two decades later, however, he lost his will to continue the struggle, in part at least because he realized that his lust for power was creating a tyranny greater than that imposed by the departed Spaniards.

In the business world, **Andrew Carnegie** was a builder: his inexhaustible energy and business acumen produced the largest and most profitable steel enterprise of its day. As a philanthropist following its sale to J.P. Morgan to create U.S. Steel, he continued with equal fervour to build educational and other institutions with the proceeds of the sale.

Josef Stalin stands out among the category of leaders in our sample who seek personal power for its own sake. Having achieved absolute power in the 1920s by outmanoeuvring all potential opponents, he then used this power to sustain his position throughout the Second World War and its aftermath. Lacking a personal vision and values which could serve as a beacon to his followers, Stalin did have direction: a relentless, compelling drive to dominate his environment. In Chapter 5, we address the issue of morality in leadership. However painful it may be to acknowledge, Stalin was an outstanding leader in our context of setting direction and motivating his followers in an environment of rapid change and conflicting forces.

Another variant of the theme of personal power is the example of **Otto von Bismarck**. Driven by an overwhelming will for power and influence, Bismarck sublimated this drive into building the German nation, on behalf of Kaiser William, into continental Europe's most powerful state.

Our leadership universe could equally have included others for whom personal power alone was the sole guiding force: Shaka Zulu (Ritter, 1955), whose inner discipline and ruthless aggrandizement built the Zulu nation of the nineteenth century, is one among many whose inclusion would replicate the profile established by Stalin.

At the other extreme are those individuals whose values constitute the substance of their leadership. Some of the most effective leaders in history have successfully aligned their personal values with those of their constituency. Thus **George Washington's** unique role as military and political leader in the nascent United States was rooted in his values, which mirrored to a remarkable extent those of his countrymen: patriotism, honesty, integrity and a commitment to the democratic process. In the wrenching split with the mother country, Washington by almost universal acclaim was given control of the colonial armies, named President of the Constituent Assembly and awarded all electoral votes in the first two presidential elections.

In another traumatic moment of American history, **Abraham Lincoln's** values during the Civil War constituted the beacon of his leadership. His honesty, integrity and commitment to consensus during a polarized civil war shaped his vision of a Union of the warring states. Whatever his personal views on slavery or the other issues, he tirelessly advocated a vision of a United States which could not be torn asunder by a single divisive issue or by the departure of its members.

Another successful soldier whose values drove his political leadership was **Oliver Cromwell**. In the turmoil of the Civil War against Charles I, Cromwell's lodestar was a godly but tolerant England in which all religious and political factions could live peacefully. Forced into a political leadership role in the vacuum following the execution of Charles, he spent the rest of his life in a frustrating struggle against extremists on all sides who sought factional advantage.

Woodrow Wilson also embodied a value-driven vision which provided his focus throughout a multi-faceted career as educator, political reformer, President and peacemaker after World War I. Himself an accomplished student of leadership, Wilson espoused a philosophy of social justice and economic opportunity which he personally elevated to a vision of world peace as he led the negotiations culminating in the Versailles Treaty. Although his values were his own, he viewed the role of political leader as one whose task was to identify and expose the often-unspoken will of the mass of the electorate.

Outside the realm of the political chieftain, values have provided the direction of a host of spiritual, public service and social leaders. **Mohandas Gandhi** evolved over his lifetime the philosophy of a community living truth through sacrifice. In the religious and political turmoil of India before World War II, Gandhi espoused the vision of a vast community living at peace, respecting the views and rights of all its members in contrast to the religious extremists on both the Hindu and Muslim sides. His steadfast commitment to this ideal earned him a remarkable moral authority for an individual with no formal political status, and the ideal of achieving truth through sacrifice has remained a moral force well after Gandhi's death in defence of his ideal.

Florence Nightingale is another leader whose commitment to values generated a level of influence well beyond any formal institutional role. Her deeply rooted sense of humanitarian values, sustained by an iron will, extended her influence from British military hospitals during the Crimean War to sanitation in British India and ultimately a host of measures to improve public health in the United Kingdom. The direction she provided became a guiding light for a host of British administrators committed to improving living standards in India, even though she never visited the sub-continent. By the same token, **Schweitzer's** reverence for life was epitomized in his total commitment to the well-being of the thousands of Africans treated at his hospital in Lambarene.

A highly successful spiritual leader was **Ignatius Loyola**, founder of the Jesuit order in the sixteenth century. Having discovered personal salvation through good works, the vow of poverty and the teachings of Jesus Christ, he then mobilized these values into a world-wide community of thousands of Jesuit missionaries committed to implement them in countries from Japan to Africa and Latin America. The direction imposed by his *Spiritual Exercises* constituted the foundation stone of what became a massive global institution.

Setting and sustaining direction is thus an essential attribute for leadership across cultures, time periods and fields of human endeavour. Showing the way in itself is , however, only the first step in the leadership process. Sustaining that direction in the face of failure and overwhelming opposition is, on the other hand, a much rarer talent. Two examples encountered in selecting our case-studies may suffice to put this achievement in perspective.

The Marquis de Lafayette (Buckman, 1977) was well placed in 1791 in the crisis of the French Revolution to emerge as a leader of the centrist, bourgeois forces. A hero of the American Revolution and highly respected despite his noble title by the revolutionary forces for his staunch republican views, Layafette as the commander of the Paris National Guard was buffeted on the left by Jacobin revolutionaries and on the right by a vacillating Louis XVI. The pressures were too much for him. Attacked by the left after firing on the crowd at the Champs de Mars in July 1791, he decided to retire to his home in the Auvergne and eschewed any active involvement in politics – thus declining an opportunity which was accepted with alacrity by Napoleon Bonaparte several years later.

A similar decision was apparently taken by Leon Trotsky in the aftermath of the disability and death of V.I. Lenin in 1924. As the military hero of the Bolshevik party and a superior intellect in the ideological debate which was to decide the future leadership of the party, Trotsky was well placed against rivals such as Stalin. Yet in the critical meeting of Bolshevik leaders which took place at Lenin's funeral, Trotsky was remarkably absent – a classical failure of will against a determined opponent.

These examples of vacillation and failure of will highlight – particularly in the context of revolutionary conflict – the central importance of disciplined direction in the leadership profile. Not only Trotsky and Lafayette, but so many others encountered in our research have vacillated when confronted with the crushing pressure of leadership in conflict. To quote Gardner, 'Leadership requires major expenditure of effort and energy – more than most people care to make!' (3). And so often the fate of our leaders – both positive and negative – has hung on the weakness of their opponents.

Thus **Bismarck's** success was tied inextricably to his ability to dominate the weak-willed Kaiser. **George Washington's** ability to remain a military threat for six years was at least in part due to the vacillations and lack of confidence of his counterparts in the British army. **Joan of Arc** was unable to pursuade the weak-willed Charles VII to support – and ultimately rescue – her following his coronation. **Hitler's** generals plotted regularly to overthrow him, but sufficient will to take action only occurred in July 1944 when the war had already been lost.

Lincoln almost lost the war by his reliance on George McClellan, whose lack of initiative and determination became legendary. San Martin permitted himself to be elbowed aside in the battle for influence in Ecuador and Peru by a more determined **Bolivar**. Finally, Enrique of Castille was unable to take effective action against **Isabella** despite her repudiation of his authority.

Referring to leadership in a revolutionary context, James MacGregor Burns believes that 'leaders must be absolutely dedicated to the cause and able to demonstrate that commitment by giving time and effort to it, risking their lives, undergoing imprisonment, exile, persecution and continual hardship' (Burns: 202). Revolutionary leadership in particular is 'passionate, dedicated, single-minded, ruthless, self-assured, courageous, tireless, usually humorless, often cruel ... its success rests on a powerful value system, a responsiveness to popular need and a systematic suppression of dissent' (239). This view is reinforced by Crane Brinton, who speaks of the 'discipline, single mindedness and centralization of authority' of the successful revolutionary leader in a struggle where ordinary people may be 'quite incapable of the mental and moral as well as physical strain of being a devoted extremist in the crisis of a revolution' (Kellerman, 1986: 225).

Providing consistent and sustained direction is, however, only the initial prerequisite in the task of achieving results through motivating others. The next two chapters describe other traits which characterize the leaders portrayed in Part I.

2 Mobilizing Support: Putting Human Insight to Work

Our second principal finding from an examination of this leadership universe is the high quality of their interpersonal skills – essentially their insight into human behaviour. The leadership profile of virtually all of the 25 individuals is marked by such insight, whether manifested in superior oratorical or debating skills, negotiating prowess, exploiting others' weaknesses, the use of ambiguity in dealing with opposing forces, or simply building relationships on the basis of trust and communication.

The use to which the leaders put their interpersonal talents varies widely, but environmental circumstances understandably play a key role. A king in a hereditary monarchy can clearly use a different interpersonal style than his counterpart in nineteenth-century America or twentieth-century France, much less a religious or humanitarian leader without any formal authority.

The literature on leadership behaviour across cultures (Bass, 1990: 34) attempts to classify national styles on the basis of traditional distinctions such as autocratic versus democratic, or participative versus directive leadership. The evidence seems to confirm some correlation between nationality and prevalence of leadership style, yet it is far from conclusive.

While most of the leaders studied are clearly more comfortable in certain of these styles than others, underpinning the choice of style is their universal success in understanding the motives of their audience and shaping their leadership behaviour on the basis of this understanding. Not only are they capable of successfully employing more than one style depending on the circumstances, but also one can imagine many of them thriving in a totally different culture.

One of the most significant findings of our research is the ability to motivate highly diverse audiences and constituencies. Left and right, rich and poor, soldiers and civilians – all can be successfully addressed by these extraordinary leaders who can empathize with them, speak to their needs and often plot a course which leads to the leader's objective.

At one pole in our sample, interpersonal skills are used by dominant personalities largely to impose their will on their followers. There is little doubt about the outcome desired by the leader, and the interests of the led are not a serious factor in his calculations. Yet, the leader must measure his or her authoritarian style against the motivation of the followers or risk being overthrown. Arguably the leadership challenge is less for the current possessor of such authority, but obtaining it in the first place usually requires the exercise of strong interpersonal skills. And history is replete with the failure of authoritarians either during their reign or, more likely, the disintegration of their achievements following their disappearance from the scene.

Perhaps the greatest gap between current leadership theory and the actual practice of our historical sample lies in this interpersonal dimension. The plethora of literature on business leadership focuses on the alignment of leader and followers in terms of values and interests. Leading authors such as Bass and Bennis describe the techniques of empowerment, communication and empathy to build a solid bond between leader and led. Aligning objectives is thus the starting point of the highly desired transcendental leadership.

Yet it is clear from our sample that many if not most leaders are motivated by their own drives for power and influence. For them, any insight into human behaviour is leveraged to their maximum personal benefit. They are fully capable of employing this insight for bullying, deceiving, terrorizing and otherwise manipulating their followers to move in the chosen direction. Whether as businessmen, politicians or institutional heads, human sensitivity is often subordinated to ego drives. Thus 'leadership can be exercised in the service of noble, liberating, enriching ends, but it can also serve to manipulate, mislead and repress' (Rosenbach: 45).

Moreover, many of the most successful leaders in our universe – in sharp contrast to the ideal depicted in current leadership literature – make little effort to bond with their closest colleagues in the leadership process. Even the most participative, collaborative leaders like Lincoln, Washington and Wilson have few intimate collaborators with whom decisions and strategies are regularly shared. And when such a group exists, as in the case of Ataturk in his formative years and Tito following victory in World War II, it often disbands as the leader finds he must lead from the front on his own responsibility. Successful leadership thus appears to be a lonely task, with the leader often obliged to take difficult decisions on his own and execute them without the support of an empowered group of close collaborators.

Thus **Alexander the Great** was able to lead his Macedonian army for a decade of successful conquest across Asia, thousands of miles from their homeland, by a combination of bribery, strict discipline and the occasional emotional appeal to personal loyalty. Well aware of the need to obtain the support of his Persian subjects in sustaining his conquests, he knowingly risked antagonizing his Greek soldiers by integrating Persian recruits into a combined army. When confronted with the inevitable resistance, he would appeal – usually with success – to their fear of the unknown in an unfriendly land as well as loyalty to him personally. As one leadership authority puts it, 'Only the remarkable personality and presence of Alexander ... could hold this flock of Greek rams and Persian she-goats together' (Adair, 1980: 68).

Peter the Great, a classic autocrat with an iron will and paternalistic approach to his subjects, nevertheless devoted considerable energy to changing their attitudes and setting a personal example of the appropriate behaviour. Aware that a Westernized Russia required competent officers and administrators, he committed himself to reorganizing the civil service and minimizing Russia's traditional corruption. **Charlemagne** faced a similar challenge in eighth century Europe. While generally imposing his patriarchal views on his vast empire, he would still carry out the traditional formality of consultation with his nobles in the form of semi-annual assemblies which would debate issues he brought before them. A skilled negotiator, he successfully won over the chieftains of opposing tribes by religious and other concessions. Meritocracy pervaded his domestic administration, which was based on a professional corps of personal representatives who functioned as his emissaries throughout the far-flung empire and were rotated to prevent them becoming too committed to a given territory.

In similar vein, a millenium later **Napoleon** supplemented his military genius with deep insight into the needs of his soldiers and the French nation in general. Skilful manipulation of the national desire for glory, the soldiers' appreciation of the award of military honours and the sensitive handling of the religious Concordat all demonstrate **Napoleon's** interpersonal skills.

Among this group of dominant leaders, perhaps the most remarkable for his insight into human motivation is **Adolf Hitler**. A skilled master of mass psychology, he carefully crafted his remarkable oratory and showmanship to win and then consolidate his power. His ability to 'respond to the vibrations of the human heart with the sensibility of a seismograph' (Bullock, 1991) brought him to power in 1933 through the established democratic electoral process. Once in power, Hitler masterfully manoeuvred for years between the conservative military and his revolutionary SA army, but he was also capable of bullying and tantrums when he felt it would achieve the desired result.

While **Andrew Carnegie** is best known for his relentless drive and ambition in building a business empire, he also had 'a most intuitive perception of the boundaries' (Wall, 1970: 290) of acceptable interpersonal behaviour with his many internal and external constituencies. Within Carnegie Steel, he established a meritocratic environment where performance was richly rewarded with company stock. With suppliers and customers he was a deft negotiator able to leverage fully his competitive advantage.

Although **Josef Stalin's** leadership was driven solely by his desire for power, he obtained that power only by years of delicate and sensitive manipulation of his rivals in the Bolshevik ranks. In a party ideologically committed to collective leadership, he emerged as sole leader in the late 1920s by remarkable dissimulation which earned him the accolade of 'master of dosage' of the poison needed to eliminate these rivals.

Another authoritarian leader who successfully blended an overpowering will with interpersonal sensitivity is **Otto von Bismarck**. His armoury – ranging from charm and humour to brutality and deceit – won over a host of opponents, from the Kaiser to foreign heads of state. In similar fashion, **Bolivar** was capable of charming constituent assemblies, recalcitrant sol-

diers, rivals for power and conquered cities – as well as terrorizing opposing forces and running roughshod over elected
bodies when he deemed it effective.

At the other end of the interpersonal spectrum are those
leaders who successfully manage change in an open, democratic environment. **Woodrow Wilson's** talents as a brilliant orator
and skilled negotiator were rooted in this unique ability to
reach out to, and understand the motives of, his audience.
Whether reforming a university curriculum or legislating a
new banking system, he prided himself on his ability to tune in
to the sensitivities of the relevant constituencies.

Charles de Gaulle, another remarkable orator with a keen
sense of his audience, was able to navigate successfully
between sharply opposed factions both in the critical days of
the 1944 Liberation and the 1958 Algerian crisis by a deft
blend of ambiguity and appeal to national interests. **Shigeru
Yoshida**, faced with the opposing interests of his Japanese electorate and the American occupational authorities, was also
obliged to resort to ambiguity – yet at the same time steadfastly pursuing his national vision.

Henri IV combined an appeal to the French national interest with his ability to relate to the masses. An inspiring soldier
who led from the front with his white-plumed helmet and
shared the battlefield conditions with his troops, he was able
to carry on a bantering dialogue with a stranger on a Paris
street as well as forcefully drive the acceptance of the Edict of
Nantes through reluctant Parliaments. **Tito** also could ingrati-
ate himself with his demanding political masters in Moscow as
well as bond in exceptional fashion with his party members
and Partisan forces – at the same time as he imposed stern discipline on both.

Among the most skilled – and patient – conciliators are two
American Presidents: **George Washington** and **Abraham
Lincoln**. Washington dealt patiently and sensitively with recalcitrant congressmen and governors, weak and unreliable generals, and mutinous and unskilled troops for an agonizing six
years as Commander-in-Chief. His deep understanding of
their needs – reinforced by his total commitment to discipline
in the national interest – held the colonial forces together
until victory in 1782.

Abraham Lincoln used a similar honesty and personal integrity to build a level of trust with the American electorate which held the country together during an extended and bloody civil war. Through his weekly 'public opinion baths' with any citizen who cared to visit the White House, as well as constant dialogue with all parties, Lincoln built a sufficient consensus on the way forward to defeat extremists on both sides of the key slavery issue. **Pericles**, committed to open democracy as an article of faith, for three decades dealt successfully in open debate with the Athenian assembly, appealing to their pride and sense of glory to persuade them to endure privation and commit resources to the empire.

Oliver Cromwell's outstanding success as a military leader was matched on the political front by a compassionate, conciliatory approach to the multitude of factions battling for influence after the death of Charles I. Demands from Royalists, Scottish nationalists, the army and religious extremists such as the Levellers were met by a leader who, as demonstrated in the Putney debates, was prepared to have dialogue and debate with all to advance his goal of a godly, tolerant England.

Another successful soldier turned statesman is **Kemal Ataturk**. At Gallipoli and in the subsequent battle with the Greeks for independence, Ataturk leveraged his knowledge of the Turkish soldier and his capabilities. A skilled communicator in the intense debate which shaped the new Turkish nation, Ataturk spent hours each day in a dialogue with his reformist colleagues and the newly formed Grand National Assembly to build a consensus on the way forward.

In the realm of social and religious reform, strong leadership has required a unique sense of human need and a rare ability to articulate these needs without the support of institutional infrastructure and a major political platform. **Florence Nightingale** thus became 'the rock to which everyone clung', not only because of her strong values and will, but also her ability to build relations of confidence and trust with key decision-makers – from Queen Victoria and her Prime Ministers to officials of the War Department, India Office and others. Not above leaking information to the media to achieve her goals, she forcefully leveraged her relationships with Lord

Herbert Stanley and others to substitute for the absence of formal authority.

Mohandas Gandhi's sensitivity to the needs and aspirations of his constituencies in South Africa and India enabled him to mobilize millions to support the strikes, fasts and marches aimed at his goal of truth through sacrifice. The force of his example in defying authority, combined with his extraordinary power to build mass support, was a central element in the process leading to Indian independence.

Ignatius Loyola also combined the force of personal example with highly sensitive antennae tuned in to the frequencies of his audience. Although totally committed personally to his doctrine of salvation, he was a good listener, able to discuss openly and acknowledge the viewpoint even of fiercely opposed groups such as the Lutherans. His ability to manage successfully the far-flung Jesuit global structure was due in no small part to his skill in matching people with assignments; he did indeed 'know each of us best'.

Finally, **Albert Schweitzer** displayed a remarkable range of persuasive skills. Not only could he win the confidence and the support of uneducated and deprived Africans, but he could also charm sophisticated Westerners by his unique sensitivity to their individual needs.

Our universe of 25 leaders thus displays a remarkable empathy to the needs of their constituencies as well as a formidable armoury of interpersonal styles to be matched with the appropriate circumstances. Whether this talent is used for 'good' (alignment and sharing of values) or 'evil' (manipulation or bullying) will be analysed in Chapter 5. In this chapter we also address the value of transcendental leadership as a benchmark in appraising leadership success.

Even the most gifted of these highly sensitized leaders, however, was vulnerable to defeat and ultimate failure. **Pericles** stumbled after three decades when his middle-of-the-road policies were overcome by military failure, while **Yoshida** was finally unable to satisfy both his US and Japanese constituencies. Others like **de Gaulle**, **Hitler** and **Napoleon** became over confident and overreached themselves.

3 Disciplined and Relentless Pursuit

The third – and perhaps most remarkable – quality of our leadership universe is its relentless, disciplined and determined pursuit of the directional goals established. Whether democrat or dictator, humanitarian or political leader, each of the leaders in the 25 case-studies rarely faltered in his or her drive, regardless of the forces arrayed against them.

While contemporary business literature admonishes would-be leaders to 'act out' their visions, 'Lead from the front!' or 'Do what you tell others to do', the actual leaders in Part I of this book go well beyond these clichés. In a word, their direction *is* their life.

Throughout the biographical material of our leadership sample, the words 'iron will', 'single-minded', 'disciplined' and 'relentless' appear on most pages. Even with their backs to the wall and facing almost certain defeat, each of them kept the faith and continued on, or even redoubling their efforts. They were regularly overtaken by physical exhaustion and illness but continued the battle. Fearless in refusing to be deflected by danger; the goal was too important compared with the risk of assassination or death on the battlefield. Not only did the military commanders lead from the front, thus sharing all the risks with their troops, but the political and social leaders also stood up at the front, both showing the way and setting an example, at the same time offering themselves as a physical target for the opposition.

The patience and persistence of these leaders is remarkable. Years, if not decades, might pass before conditions were appropriate for them to assume a leadership role, yet they threw themselves into this role, whenever it is offered, with their original direction unimpaired. While torn internally with frustration and occasionally with self-doubt, to the outside world they were seen to maintain their steadfast determination.

The inevitable corollary of this overwhelming drive was the placing of heavy demands on others as well as themselves.

Expectations of followers and family were high, and there tended to be little sympathy for even close colleagues who could not meet these expectations. Impatience and stubbornness are charges frequently levelled at the leaders in our selection.

Among military leaders, disciplined execution is understandably of central importance. Those in our study truly lived up to the precept of 'leading from the front' to maintain the bond of trust with those whose lives were at stake. John Keegan holds that 'the first and greatest imperative of command is to be present in person. Those who impose risk must be seen to share it'. (Syrett and Hogg: 43).

Among the military and political leaders, the energy and drive of **Peter the Great** are legendary. Fighting a 21-year war with Sweden, transforming St Petersburg from a captured marsh into a splendid capital city, continually touring his massive country to inspect his major projects personally, Peter drove change in the most intimate fashion. By the same token, with his childhood shaped by the terrors of military revolt, his iron will brooked no opposition, and he was ruthless in eliminating even the possibility of this opposition, to the extent of driving his own son to his death.

Alexander the Great's energy and determination were equally impressive. Prepared to commit seven months to the capture of a single city (Tyre), and spend three years in the inhospitable Afghan mountains to destroy the last vestige of Persian resistance, he yielded to his army's plea to return to the west only when it was clear that, after 17 000 miles and eight years, they had had enough. Another indomitable chieftain is **Charlemagne,** whose ruthless pursuit of a Christian kingdom found him at the age of 62 still commanding his armies in a relentless 32-year war against Saxon tribes and criss-crossing his vast empire to put down local revolts. A tireless administrator, he personally prepared hundreds of capitularies, or orders, which set out in exhaustive detail the way forward for the empire.

Another Western ruler remarkable for the strength of her will and determination in the service of her vision of a united, Catholic Spain is **Isabella of Castile**. Shaped in the turmoil of a divided country, she imposed her will on her predecessor as well as her husband Ferdinand and personally dealt with fractious subjects. A classic workaholic, she acted as quartermaster general to support the armies of her husband and personally set up tribunals throughout Castile to resolve local disputes.

Josef Stalin's iron determination lived up to the *nom de guerre* of 'steel' by which he was known since his revolutionary days. Having forged this determination as a revolutionary, including three years in painful exile in Siberia, in the 1920s he methodically set about assuming a degree of control of his environment, to an extent which eventually became paranoid. Another determined communist was **Josip Tito**. Taking his life in his hands before World War II both in Moscow during Stalinist purges and as an undercover agent in Yugoslavia pursued by the royalist government, during the war Tito continued faithful to his goals although facing the might of the *Wehrmacht*.

Joan of Arc's single-minded pursuit of her vision in the brief year of her political activity placed her at the front of her troops and led to her eventual capture at Compiègne. For a full year as a captive she kept faith with her vision despite oppressive physical and mental pressures, giving way at the end only in sight of her executioners.

Having articulated his vision of German resurrection in the early 1920s, **Adolf Hitler** clung to it until final defeat with the Russian armies entering Berlin. In the process he elevated will-power to an ideal in itself, a national virtue, which sustained him for years in the delicate negotiations with various factions prior to winning office in 1933.

Personally committed to an alliance with the major Western powers, **Shigeru Yoshida** as a pre-war Japanese diplomat fought unsuccessfully for peace against his government's policy. During World War II, he led a group openly committed to peace and was subsequently arrested for his views.

Our universe includes a number of military leaders whose success on the battlefield propelled them into political power, where they displayed the same energy, determination and discipline which had won battlefield success. **Henri IV**, whose charismatic military leadership ('follow me; do what you see me do') produced an unbroken string of victories, committed himself in both peace and war to a tolerant France. Prepared to wait patiently five years after assuming the crown before entering his capital, he agonized over the question of giving up his

Protestant faith – less because of any personal commitment but because it might send a message of vacillation to his followers. **Napoleon** was another successful French general who assumed political power in troubled times. An acknowledged workaholic, he was also sufficiently disciplined to leave the woman he loved in the hope of producing an heir to the throne.

Another commander with an unbeaten record who had to deal with the challenges of peacetime opposition was **Oliver Cromwell**, who took political power with some reluctance in the vacuum created by the execution of Charles. Living a vision of a godly, tolerant England was not an easy task, and Cromwell was beset by inner doubt and the difficulty of building consensus in a polarized country. Yet he persisted in his efforts to bring together the various factions and weld a consensus in successive parliaments.

George Washington was another successful soldier who reluctantly accepted the challenge of political leadership. Having triumphed on the battlefield by his total discipline and commitment to the national cause, he applied the same values to an increasingly fractious United States polarizing between Federalists and Republicans. While increasingly unhappy in this role, his persistent pursuit of the middle ground and focus on the national interest held the country together at a formative period of its evolution.

Forced into exile three times, **Simon Bolivar** on each occasion assembled a new force and returned to attack the Spanish army in Venezuela. **Charles de Gaulle's** uncompromising will was an integral part of his leadership with both Allies, opponents and other political forces. The exercise of this will in the critical moments of defeat in 1940, liberation in 1944, and the Algerian crisis in 1958 was matched when he resigned initially in 1946 and finally in 1968 when he felt he could exercise authority no longer.

Pericles' determination to sustain democracy was sufficiently disciplined for him to allow himself to be outvoted – and eventually thrown from office – without complaint, much less an effort to save himself by undemocratic means. Arguably his unwillingness to compromise over the Megarian embargo finally brought about his downfall.

Among political leaders without a military background – and therefore without the ability to establish their authority on the battlefield – **Abraham Lincoln** and **Woodrow Wilson** stand out in the forceful, determined exercise of their values. Always conciliatory and consistent in his pursuit of the federal Union, **Lincoln** endured repeated military defeat by his commanders, the slanders of his opponents attacking the 'Gorilla President', and constant political intrigues to win final victory. In the depths of despair in August 1864 after years of apparently fruitless conflict with the rebels threatening Washington, he was truly prepared to die at his post.

Wilson's energetic leadership, in his own words, required going to the limits of complete self-sacrifice in pursuit of his ideals. A negotiator well known for his ability to keep a steady pressure to achieve results, he boldly committed himself to lead the peace negotiations after World War I, an exhausting task which ultimately broke his health and led to the defeat of the League of Nations legislation.

Another tireless, relentless democratic leader was **Kemal Ataturk**, whose tenacity in the face of external and internal strife in the formative months of the Turkish Republic represented the difference between success and failure. Having led his own troops from the front in early conflicts, in Ankara he positioned himself for hours on end at the telegraph office directing his forces, followed by equally demanding debate and discussion in the legislature.

Andrew Carnegie's legendary energy and ruthless drive was evident in both his business career and his subsequent period as a philanthropist. Relentlessly driving his colleagues to improve profitability and build market power, he applied the same spirit in parcelling out his fortune: 'tenacity and steady sailing to the haven.' **Otto von Bismarck** displayed the same tireless energy in building the new German state. Confronted with opposition on every side, he relentlessly crushed domestic opposition and weakened or conquered neighbouring states.

Ignatius Loyola's discipline refused to accept external constraints, whether threats to his health and safety or the propagation of his doctrine embodied in the *Spiritual Exercises*. Convinced that his personal leadership was central to the successful execution of the Jesuits' global mission, he managed the affairs of thousands of his missionaries around the globe with only a single secretary to assist in transmitting literally thousands of communications to and from the field.

Florence Nightingale's determination to live her humanitarian values was equally impressive. Having studied hospital reform in secret at home for eight years because of parental opposition, she overcame opposition to reform in wartime Crimea in the 1850s by patient observation of military regulations until the virtues of her approach became evident. Her health broken by round-the-clock work under primitive conditions in the Crimea, she continued her humanitarian career for another forty years in London as a semi-invalid.

Self-sacrifice in the service of his personal values was elevated by **Mohandas Gandhi** to an integral dimension of his life's work. Having suffered physical beatings as a strike leader in South Africa, he deliberately exposed his life in the fratricidal conflict in India between Hindus and Muslims which ultimately led to his assassination. Insisting on participating in every aspect of his vision of truth through sacrifice, he was active in all dimensions of life on the *ashram* – including cleaning the latrines – as well as carrying on a massive correspondence and unending series of meetings with outsiders. Finally, **Albert Schweitzer** committed all his energies until the age of 90 to the hospital community in Lambarene. His determination to sustain standards he felt essential was seen by critics as overbearing and egotistical; to him it was an integral dimension of his leadership.

What emerges from this chapter is the leader committed *à l'outrance* – to the limit of his or her energies. This does not exclude compromises and manoeuvring as long as they are consistent with the ultimate direction. But they can earn the leader the reputation for stubbornness and impatience. Worse, they can lead to death in battle, by assassination or sheer exhaustion.

4 The Profile and Impact of Leadership

The findings in the previous three chapters confirm that there is indeed a universal paradigm of leadership which extends across cultures, historical time and dimensions of human activity. Individual expertise in a specific professional dimension, such as military genius, business acumen or sheer brainpower, clearly plays a role, but in mobilizing thousands or millions over an extended period of time there is a basic commonality of leadership talents. The three key dimensions of direction, interpersonal skills and ruthless pursuit of the direction chosen are ubiquitous and shape the leader's ability to motivate his followers and achieve sustainable results.

While our selection of 25 leaders is far from a fully satisfying sample across the full three-dimensional universe, there is sufficient commonality of the profile derived from this mosaic to serve as the basis for the conclusions which follow in this and subsequent chapters.

Our findings thus broadly confirm the contemporary paradigm of business or institutional leadership in which the leader articulates a vision or distant objective, mobilizes the commitment of the relevant followers or colleagues, and lives the vision in his or her daily work. This model is perhaps best encapsulated in Kouzes and Posner's phrase 'V.I.P.: Vision, involvement and persistence' (1987: 7). As indicated in Chapters 1 and 2, however, the global paradigms of vision and involvement differ in important respects from the contemporary model of the successful business leader.

Our research also enables us to sharpen our focus on the personal traits which distinguish truly superior leadership. The contemporary literature of how-to-do-it leadership texts generates an overwhelming array of qualities which the model leader should possess. Often quite contradictory, such laundry lists are totally unrealistic in the real world of individuals struggling against a host of opposing forces imposed by multiple constituencies. Syrett and Hogg aptly put it: 'executives who are focused yet multi-faceted, self-confident yet humble, competitive yet collaborative, ethical yet pragmatic – seems a very tall order' (1992: 68).

The real world is not quite so neatly arrayed, and many of our successful leaders are individuals who have some quite unattractive and unpalatable qualities. Quite apart from those with a bent towards such pleasures of the flesh as sex and alcohol, there are those such as Bismarck, Charlemagne, Bolivar and Isabella who are quite prepared to run roughshod over opposition in pursuit of their goals – not to speak of Hitler and Stalin who are totally rejected by many historians as leaders because of their willingness to liquidate millions of followers to attain their personal goals. After reading the biographies of such individuals, one is inclined to agree with writers such as Bailey, for whom 'leaders are often villains ... it is very difficult to be an effective leader and at the same time a good person' (quoted in Syrett and Hogg: 155). Gardner agrees: 'The judgements one makes of a leader must be multidimensional, taking into consideration great strengths, streaks of mediocrity, and perhaps great flaws' (Gardner: 8)

Of particular interest is the model of military leadership which emerges from the soldiers among our universe. In an environment in which a successful leader may mean the difference between life and death for the individual follower, leadership skills understandably are highly valued. Most of the military men and women in our selection are well endowed with the professional skills which make a great commander: decisive boldness, insight into enemy behavior, imagination and flexibility, courage under pressure and tactical prowess. Yet each also had impressive generic leadership skills. Alexander the Great's empathy with his troops enabled him to keep the army together for a decade away from their homeland. Henri IV's ability to lead from the front was an integral part of his leadership success. And both Cromwell and Washington were able to quell potential mutineers by their appeal to shared values as well as discipline.

Among the three basic leadership traits of direction, disciplined execution of this direction, and interpersonal skills to motivate others to follow, the last is arguably the most interesting in a universal context. In an authoritarian environment of, say, an autocratic eighteenth-century Russia or eighth-century

Frankland, interpersonal skills and their use to motivate a nation may not appear as critical as in pluralistic, democratic nineteenth-century America, twentieth-century France or democratic Athens at the height of its power.

Yet most of the leaders in our assemblage possess motivational skills and human insight which could be adapted to a variety of external circumstances. They are truly men and women for many, if not all, seasons. Charlemagne could be a ruthless general, yet he displayed a deft sense in negotiations with his nobles and foreign chieftains. Peter the Great was equally ruthless in quelling opposition, but he patiently tried to motivate his bureaucrats and subjects to build a meritocratic Russia. Adolf Hitler's bombast with his weaker opponents could alternate with skilful persuasion of the key military and government figures who held the key to obtaining power legally in 1933. Charles de Gaulle could be a 'prince of deception' in the 1958 Algerian negotiations or an orator appealing to the highest national instincts of his countrymen.

In sum, there is solid evidence that many successful leaders in a totalitarian environment not only display strong interpersonal skills in obtaining and consolidating power, but also that in a more democratic culture they might also have thrived by the skilled employment of this same human insight.

Yet the overwhelming impression from an examination of this universe of 25 leaders is the limitations of leadership in an environment of severe conflict. A single individual can indeed change the course of events by leading others, but doing so consistently over an extended period of time is a rare achievement. Surveying the wreckage on the leadership battlefield of the 1980s, Christopher Lorenz of the *Financial Times* acknowledged that 'few leaders, either in business or in politics, last more than a decade (Syrett: 103).

The leaders selected in our research are truly exceptional individuals. In studying the course of their leadership, one is struck by the number of their contemporaries who lacked the core skills, were unable to repeat initial successes, or were swept away by events beyond their influence. By evaluating the success or ultimate failure of each of the 25 leaders one can perhaps best appreciate the power of the opposing forces they faced.

The first hurdle is simply one of longevity. Building or rescuing a nation, a major business firm or a religious movement can require decades of steadfast commitment by the leader. Yet many are cut down prematurely by the massive emotional and physical pressures generated by the external conflict.

Quite apart from the heavy day-in, day-out pressures over an extended period of time, the emotions inherent in conflict arouse and motivate assassins who target the leader as a symbol of the enemy. Thus Abraham Lincoln, Henri IV, and Mohandas Gandhi each fell victim to extremists who were prepared to sacrifice themselves to eliminate a hated opponent. The risk of assassination would appear to be an integral dimension of the leadership profile of virtually all of our subjects. For them, being physically and emotionally close to their followers or electorate, leading from the front in both military and civilian conflict, overshadows in importance the possibility – even the probability – of physical danger. The reader of these biographies emerges with a much greater appreciation of the task facing the security services charged with the physical security of their leaders!

Apart from the danger of assassination, there is the impact of emotional and physical stress on the human body. Woodrow Wilson's collapse from a stroke is an example of a leader physically overwhelmed by the pressures and tensions of conflict. The burden of carrying on intense negotiations over the post-World War I settlement with both the Allies in Paris and Republican leaders in Washington, coupled with an exhausting whistle-stop tour of the country to win voter support, was simply too much for his body to bear.

Another hurdle is a change in circumstances or environment. It is a remarkable leader who can repeat his success in a variety of different roles. For example, several of our case-studies involve successful military leaders who as civilians found themselves playing a dominant political role which placed totally different demands on their leadership talents. Thus George Washington found his role as civilian President increasingly uncomfortable as the split between Jeffersonian Republicans and Hamiltonian Federalists widened. Personally sensitive to criticism and not a talented debater or orator, he welcomed a retirement which removed him from the growing wave of personal abuse and factional conflict that marked his second term of office. By the same token, Oliver Cromwell's string of military victories contrasts sharply with the frustration of building consensus within a succession of elected Parliaments; he must have welcomed the opportunity to leave the interminable debates in Parliament for the battlefield where results could be clearly measured and achieved.

Another case of a frustrated soldier is Joan of Arc. Once she had achieved her goal of crowning Charles at Reims, she found herself relegated to supporting a weak king who had no particular role for her and, when she was captured, made little effort to rescue her. Bolivar made no pretence about his total lack of interest in actually managing the countries he conquered. Napoleon is one of the few generals turned managers who truly thrived on both military and civil challenges.

In the business world, Andrew Carnegie carried all before him in his overwhelming drive to build an industrial empire. Yet he derived much less satisfaction as a philanthropist and peace advocate, a role in which the presence of multiple constituencies, all less susceptible to his brand of vigorous dynamism, was a regular source of frustration.

Adolf Hitler was another leader unable to adapt to a changed environment. Having consolidated his power and astonished the world by a series of successful bold initiatives in the 1935–41 period, he provoked a global war which could only be won by solid, determined military leadership. In this environment his leadership style actually detracted from the efforts of his generals.

For Otto von Bismarck, the changed environment was a new Kaiser, who resented the presence of an all-powerful adviser and simply dismissed him so as to be able to exercise power himself. In the case of Shigeru Yoshida, the growing tension between American demands on Japan and increasing resistance by both right and left factions in Japan made it impossible even for a leader of Yoshida's skills to bridge the gap.

Not only do circumstances change, but the leaders themselves may evolve over time. The exercise of power has a remarkable effect on the self-image and behaviour of many. A growing self-confidence – if not arrogance – and increasing distance from the aspirations and motives of the followership are some of the occupational hazards of leadership.

Perhaps the classic case of such alienation in our selection is the example of Charles de Gaulle. Having displayed great sensitivity in dealing with the various national interests in resolving the Algerian crisis and rebuilding the French economy, de Gaulle was preoccupied with his own national agenda when the unexpected student revolt in 1968 broke his nerve. Determined to proceed with a referendum which had little relationship with the primary concerns of his countrymen, he went down to expected defeat and retired for the last time from public life.

Another case of possible overreaching by a successful leader is Woodrow Wilson's campaign for the League of Nations legislation which ultimately caused his debilitating stroke. Having thrust himself into the centre of the post-war settlement and elevated world peace to his primary aim, he committed himself to this lofty goal which, however, was of less concern to the electorate than the problems of building a peacetime economy. Had he retained his health, this bold initiative might well have succeeded, yet it can be argued that a leader more in tune with his electorate would not have taken the risk. Burns summarizes the ultimate frustration of this distinguished leader: 'to few men are given the opportunity to demonstrate the kind of leadership they had called for at the lectern, and few men – even for a time – have acquitted themselves as well as Wilson did. But in the end he was defeated by the very forces of fragmentation and mutual frustration that he had attacked – and by his own hubris.' (Burns: 166)

Despite these obstacles, however, a number of the leaders in our universe died peacefully in their 60s and 70s – or later – after decades of success in dealing with conflict in its various forms. Ignatius Loyola was able to launch the Jesuit order not only in terms of theological doctrine but also global organization and structure. Josef Stalin ruthlessly eliminated internal opposition, survived the invasion by a superior power, and skilfully leveraged his negotiating power against his post-war allies. Tito died peacefully, having garnered world-wide fame for his achievements, well before Yugoslavia came apart in the 1990s. Having created the Turkish state, Kemal Ataturk successfully managed the change process to realize his ideal of a secular, democratic and Westernized state. Isabella of Castile ruled long enough to ensure that her creation of a Catholic, united Spain would eventually become reality. And Albert Schweitzer's hospital survives as a functioning unit to this day.

Another conclusion from this research is that a leader's most significant contribution may well be felt only after his or her departure from the scene. Thus Joan of Arc played a leadership role for only a year of her young life, yet the values she represents for France have long survived her death at the stake. While Abraham Lincoln occupied the American Presidency for a fraction of the time of many of his peers, his honesty, commitment to the Union and eloquence in articulating its values have become a national tradition. Periclean democracy has become an icon for some, anathema to others. And Mohandas Gandhi's commitment to sacrifice and peaceful resistance continue to be invoked by protest groups throughout the world. Finally, Bismarck is accused by some of being ultimately responsible for World Wars I and II – simply by having created a powerful state with a strong military tradition.

In conclusion, one emerges from this analysis with a heightened appreciation for leadership in the perpetual struggle against conflicting forces. It is rare to find individuals with a passionate, totally disciplined attachment to values and vision. It is even more difficult to match these talents with the requisite human sensitivity and interpersonal skills needed to motivate others to follow in the same direction. And it is an even greater challenge to find such individuals prepared to sacrifice their personal lives and safety to pursue the public life and endure the abuse and criticism which usually is directed at them from all sides. One can well understand the feelings of a Lafayette or Trotsky who decides that, whatever his leadership potential, he prefers a quiet life.

And even if one retains the commitment, all this is not enough. One must be patient and grasp the opportunity presented by circumstances. Winston Churchill and Charles de Gaulle thus waited in the wings for years before their brand of leadership was in demand, while Shigeru Yoshida would have ended his career on retirement in 1938, had not circumstances in 1946 dictated otherwise.

In the course of this odyssey through the leadership universe, a host of images come to mind of the archetypal leader, such as a mountain climber leading his colleagues to the top, or a general leading his troops over the enemy ramparts. The image of a sailor fixing and maintaining his course has been mentioned earlier. Yet the one which remains in the author's memory is that of the swimmer crossing the English Channel: setting out to reach a fixed point far away; beset by tides, cold and fatigue which may throw him off course; and compelled to move resolutely forward against all obstacles without resting or else fail in his mission. Not many swimmers wish to undertake the task.

5 The Moral Dimension: Leadership for What?

Of all the leadership issues raised by our research, placing a moral judgement on a leader's contribution is the most divisive and least resolved. The widely different definitions of leadership cited in the Introduction demonstrate the polarization of views. We have defined leadership in this book as the proven ability over a significant period of time to achieve results through people, which may require motivating them to change their behaviour to produce the desired result. Leadership in this context is thus a means to an end.

Others, however, interpret leadership as both the means and the end. Burns articulates best such a moral, or value-based, view of leadership. 'The test of their leadership is their contribution to change, measured by purpose drawn from collective motives and values' (Burns: 427). Thus 'leaders must face the test of whether they have indeed tapped the authentic needs of followers;' (460). In this view, Gandhi is the archetypal transforming leader who 'seeks to satisfy higher needs and engage the full person of the follower' (4).

Some take a more pragmatic view. For Jennings, 'men who make history must have purpose' (Jennings, 1960: 70). For Sidney Hook, the event-making man is an outstanding individual who influences by virtue of what he is, not just what he does. In his view, 'we must rule out as irrelevant the conception of the hero as a morally worthy man ... only the making of history concerns us here' (Kellerman, 1986: 25).

From these disparate views come equally divergent opinions of whether men like Hitler, Mao Tse-tung and Stalin were tyrants or leaders. Those like the author who define leadership as a means to an end must accept that these individuals did indeed display superior leadership skills, while value-based definitions might relegate them to the lower regions of manipulators, tyrants and authoritarians.

However one defines leadership, the value judgement must eventually be made. Sooner or later the battle must be joined as to whether a leader's contribution truly met the followers' real needs, enhanced their values, or simply increased general human welfare in their time. Making such Solomonic judgements – especially when many constituences are involved – is perhaps the best argument for defining leadership as we have done, simply as a means, a mix of personal qualities and skills. At least by separating means from ends, the student of leadership can address two quite different issues: did he obtain tangible results through people, and secondly were these results positive for the people involved. In this chapter we therefore confront the leader's impact on such key values as justice, freedom, equality and prosperity.

It is in this judgemental realm that honest men can disagree honestly. This is the food and drink of contemporary political debate. Contemporary demands for a stronger leader, attacks on perceived weak leadership, and criticism of someone in a leadership position thus usually refer to the end result rather than the means. Implicit in attacks on 'our leadership' is often criticism of the leader's failure to move in the direction desired by the advocate. In Gardner's words, 'we cry out for leadership … there is an element of wanting to be rescued, of wanting a parental figure who will set all things right' (xi).

The objective of this chapter is therefore to address the issue of how to evaluate the end result of the leader's efforts. If one accepts that leadership capability is a means to an end, how can one judge the value of his or her efforts? Can one speak of good or bad leadership?

Among the plethora of efforts to categorize or classify types of leadership, one of the most useful is that of Burns. In his pathfinding book *Leadership* he distinguishes between transactional leadership, which involves day-to-day trade-offs in the dialogue between leader and follower, and transcendental leadership, which addresses the follower's true interests and values and attempts to satisfy these higher needs as described above.

While this distinction has value, it does not resolve the ultimate issue of evaluating the leader's performance. The implication is that a transactional leader may be effective in a short term situation but lack the vision needed to transform the well-being of his followership. Yet our case studies have shown that leaders like Wilson and Ataturk can be adept in the give-

and-take of daily trade-offs yet also possess a vision which aims at transforming their nation. So many in our universe can not only deal successfully with many constituencies, but also perform transactional and transformational acts concurrently. The leadership animal is sufficiently complex to defy such a distinction in the real world. As Jennings points out, an effective leader needs to be protean. 'Great leaders are many men in one' (1960: 106). We have seen among our subjects individuals such as Bismarck, Charlemagne and Hitler employ a vast repertoire of leadership styles to achieve their goals. Another multi-faceted leader is Franklin Roosevelt, who Burns quotes as 'persuading, flattering, juggling, improvising, reshuffling, harmonizing, conciliating and manipulating' (Burns, 1978: 393) to achieve results which were both transactional and transforming.

More important, the presence of a transforming vision or strong values is no guarantee that they are in the interest of those being transformed. As we shall discuss below, Gandhi's vision of living a life of truth through sacrifice was clearly a worthy goal in the interests of the nascent Indian nation, while Hitler's transforming view of the Thousand Year Reich was a disaster for the German people.

Addressing this issue in the context of the 25 leaders in our universe produces only one response to the issue of morality. Each leader's achievements, vision or no vision, transactions or no transactions, must be evaluated in the light of the interests of the followership community. This will inevitably be a subjective judgement, and, as indicated below, in many cases the judgement may be finely balanced. Often there are a host of constituencies involved in this value judgement, and the answer may be a function of which subset's interests are under the microscope.

Applying this approach to our selection of leaders produces some fairly clear judgements as well as some that are not so straightforward. Turning first to the four humanitarian leaders, the balance of evidence is in favour of a positive judgement of the efforts of Florence Nightingale, Ignatius Loyola, Albert Schweitzer and Mohandas Gandhi to improve the spiritual and material life of their constituencies. Each of these remarkable individuals was truly a servant of his or her followers in subordinating the leader's personal ambition and welfare to that of the communities they served. While ruthless in driving themselves to their goals, they all retained a personal tolerance and understanding of the weaknesses of their followers. More important, while they reserved for themselves the choice of the end and means of their reform programmes, the welfare of the followers was foremost in the leader's mind. Thus Gandhi himself decided when and for what to strike or fast, and Loyola imposed his Spiritual Exercises as the framework for his followers' studies, but the decisions were consciously taken in the perceived interest of the follower. Schweitzer only rarely permitted his initial judgement to be altered when it came to managing 'his hospital'.

In the business domain, the value contributed by Andrew Carnegie is also fairly easily determined. In a reasonably competitive world where long-term financial success usually stems from value provided to customers, the bottom-line profit is a fairly good measure of performance. While the free-wheeling business environment of post-Civil War America may have had its anti-competitive aspects, Carnegie Steel did produce a competitive product and generated outstanding returns for its stockholders. On the debit side, however, Carnegie must forever carry the stigma of ultimate responsibility for the deaths in 1892 at the Homestead strike attributable to his ruthless efforts to reduce union influence.

Applying a value judgement to the leadership results of many of the political leaders in our sample is also relatively uncontroversial. In the United States, Abraham Lincoln and George Washington not only shared core values with most of their fellow citizens but, more importantly, regarded themselves as the servants of these citizens. Hence their unending efforts to build consensus, discuss and debate issues, and focus on national goals which transcended factional interests. Woodrow Wilson was a reformer who did not hesitate to drive change over opposing forces. Yet his touchstone was always a vision of social justice and economic opportunity to which he subordinated his personal ambitions.

In Periclean Athens, its citizens did enjoy a remarkably high standard of physical and intellectual prosperity. While the empire's subjects and opponents may have a different view, Pericles' vision for three decades did indeed make Athenian citizenship a true privilege.

Kemal Ataturk and Henri IV are also examples of strong leaders whose direction was determined by a vision of their nation which transcended their personal goals. Henri was prepared to concede his deeply held religious views – and risk the fury of his Protestant followers – in the interests of a state which tolerated all religions.

The case of Ataturk is somewhat more complex. He steadfastly drove his emerging country toward the ideal of a Westernized state with a secular, democratic foundation. As the external threat receded and the consensus established by his original band of followers eroded, Ataturk was capable of driving his will over opposition in the elected legislature. His personal power clearly could have been turned to advance his own personal agenda or that of another faction. Yet until his death he remained loyal to a vision in which different views could be debated freely. Arguably the strength of democratic forces in Turkey today can be attributed to this liberal commitment.

Evaluating Tito and Napoleon also produces light as well as shadow. Tito did indeed bring the disparate elements of his unruly nation together, defeat the invading Germans and introduce some reform into the Stalinist economic model. Yet it was done at great cost to individual liberties, and the subsequent disintegration of the Yugoslav nation both enhances his own leadership performance and rationalizes the view that it was all for naught.

Napoleon likewise made a lasting and positive contribution to a French nation emerging from the darkness of ineffective monarchical rule. By the same token, many of the nations he conquered arguably may owe him a debt of gratitude. But the decimation on the battlefield and the dislocation of the European economy in the early 1800s must be added to the debit side of the balance sheet.

At the other extreme of the value spectrum, a number of political leaders were pursuing personal ambitions which had little to do with the interests of most of the constituencies involved. Whatever Stalin may have articulated about the virtues of a dictatorship of the proletariat or Hitler on the subject of German resurrection and renewal, the net impact of their leadership for their countries was disastrous. By implicitly assuming that the national interest was identical to their own, their leadership led to the death by combat, execution, exile and starvation of millions of their own citizens as well as unfortunate foreigners who got in the way. Arguably the only beneficiaries of their leadership were a small coterie of their followers as well as themselves personally.

Much the same can be said about Alexander the Great, the classic conqueror. In pursuing his personal ambition to conquer the entire Persian Empire, he may have enriched his army from the vast treasure of the Persians, but it is difficult to detect much net value from the slaughter of armies, the plundering of cities and the building of an impressive military force.

By the same token, Bolivar's vision of an independent continental nation produced little benefit for its citizens, who arguably were better off under Spanish rule. At least Bolivar's hero Napoleon had made some effort to manage his conquests for the benefit of their citizens. The reader of Bolivar's history cannot escape the conclusion that one of the principal motives for his voluntary retirement in 1830 was the recognition of this failure.

Evaluating the contribution of several of the monarchs in our sample is a more complex task. Thus Isabella of Castile certainly achieved a more united, peaceful kingdom from the relative anarchy of her predecessors, which presumably added to the well-being of the mass of her subjects. Yet her relentless pursuit of the Moorish kingdom in Granada, the expulsion of the Moors and Jews and above all her sponsorship of the Inquisition led to death, exile, and persecution for a large number of her subjects. In evaluating the results of her passion to create a Catholic Spain, the judgement understandably differs depending on whether one is a Jew, a Muslim or a Catholic. And even in the case of the latter, Isabella regularly overrode complaints from the Pope that she was overzealous in pursuing the Inquisition.

A mixed judgement is also called for in the case of Peter the Great, another autocrat who defined the national interest in terms of his personal vision. On the positive side of the balance, Peter laid the groundwork for a more efficient state capable of achieving the benefits of the contemporary Western democracies. Yet the proportion of gross national product devoted to the building of St Petersburg – as well as a military machine used to expand the empire at the expense of the Turks – was gigantic.

By the same token, Charlemagne's remarkable achievement in creating the Holy Roman Empire was a mixed blessing for his subjects, in particular the neighbours he conquered. The pagan Saxons may have represented a real threat to his vision of a united, Christian empire in Europe, but the 32 years of warfare – not to speak of the massacre of thousands of Saxons at Verden attributable to his pique – was a considerable burden to the people. Yet Charlemagne's ability to create a well-managed, peaceful and united empire stands out like a beacon in the darkness of that particular period in Western history.

Another mixed blessing is Bismarck's creation, by peaceful as well as violent means, of modern Germany. Once again, the judgement may depend on one's point of view: a German businessman or soldier benefiting from a more powerful single market, or a German prince obliged to surrender his autonomy. Blaming Bismarck for the subsequent disasters of William II and Hitler may be going too far, but Bismarck played a central role in creating a state whose power and mentality could be turned in such an aggressive direction.

On the other hand, Yoshida's rebuilding of a Japanese state consistent with its conservative tradition, yet intimately linked to an alliance with democratic America is a signal achievement of benefit to almost all the relevant constituencies. While the political structure he created has its defects – some of which are only being addressed four decades later – it is difficult to contemplate an alternative more in the interest of Japan and its neighbours.

Given the number of leaders driven by power and other personal objectives, the obvious question is how the follower – or the student of leadership – can evaluate the direction pursued by the leader. Will his lust for power destroy a nation, as did Hitler or Stalin, or will the result be more balanced, as was the case with Charlemagne and Bismarck? The task is made more difficult by the leader's talent for ambiguity and skill in masking his ultimate motives.

It is beyond the scope of this book to provide a thoughtful and comprehensive response to that question. Yet our analysis does indicate that the clear direction which is such an integral part of the leadership process should give some indication to potential followers of the leader's ultimate goal. This does not have to be as explicit as Hitler's *Mein Kampf,* but an objective observer should be able to evaluate the likely benefits and dangers. At a relatively early stage of their leadership development, power-driven individuals such as Stalin, Bolivar, Alexander, Bismarck and Carnegie made it reasonably clear that they would continue to thrust forward in their chosen direction until met by a countervailing or superior force.

The communications explosion of the late twentieth century, coupled with the spread of pluralistic political systems with their accompanying panoply of media exposure and opposition platforms, provides a powerful searchlight with which objective observers can judge the leader's contribution to such key follower values as economic wealth, personal freedom, justice and equity. Followers and opponents may be won over by a leader such as Hitler, but the increasingly well-informed observer can discern the basic trends. The trade-offs may be complex – say, between economic growth and personal freedom, or minority rights and the national interest – and making a balanced appraisal invariably requires personal judgement. Yet the student of leadership should be capable of evaluating the evidence and formulating a balanced appraisal – hopefully in time to avoid a repetition of disasters such as World Wars I and II.

6 Conclusions for Leadership Today

The goal of this chapter is to address one of the original questions which provided the genesis for this book. What can we learn from the lessons of history that is relevant today, at the end of the twentieth century, with particular reference to the violent conflicts which have set men and nations against each other in recent memory? What indeed can be the role of the individual leader in resolving these conflicts? Does the profile of leaders through the centuries give us any useful insight into how a potential leader might proceed?

Leaders active in the final decades of this century have been excluded from our sample, partly because of the continuing role many still play on the political stage, but also because objective, quality biographies delving deeply into the leadership practice of the relevant individuals are in short supply. Our universe of 25 leaders has identified many whose contribution could only be fairly measured decades, if not longer, after their death when partisan rivalries had faded and subsequent generations could put the leader in perspective. Yet a thoughtful reader of contemporary journals obtains some insight into the successes and failures of leaders during the last quarter of this century, and the observations below are derived largely from such general reading without the benefit of interviews or biographical reading.

During the past few decades, sharp and polarized conflict has taken a number of forms. First, religious, ethnic and national schism has rent society in the Indian subcontinent, sub-Saharan Africa, Palestine, Northern Ireland, as well as the former Yugoslavia and other countries. Second, within a given nation, polarized factions have proliferated; the right–left conflict in Central and Latin America is perhaps the most prevalent form of political schism. The break up of the Soviet empire in the 1990s has created a particular subset of traumatic conflict in the former Soviet Union. Finally, in both mature and developing economies, the challenge of disciplined allocation of scarce resources to maximize economic growth has created another level of conflict among factions fighting for their share of the economic pie. Maintaining political leadership while providing steady, real economic growth is one of the most demanding challenges of our time.

We address first the violent, armed conflicts stemming from polarized national, ethnic and religious forces. In recent memory, such conflicts in Northern Ireland, Palestine, Afghanistan, the Lebanon, and the former Yugoslavia have ground on for years, if not decades, despite the efforts of well-meaning leaders on all sides, plus outside mediators, to build a reasonable consensus on a peaceful way forward. To repeat the query raised in Chapter 1, are these forces simply too strong to be resolved by effective leadership, or do these unhappy regions simply lack the requisite leadership talents?

The balance of evidence is that the former is the case. For 25 years, the conflict in Northern Ireland boiled on despite the efforts of many of its own citizens to stop the bloodshed and the commitment of successive British and Irish leaders to hold the ring while negotiating a compromise which would be acceptable to the two major factions. In 1995, such a solution finally appears within reach. Several leaders in the Northern Irish community have clearly played a major role in bringing the protagonists together, but the outside observer is aware that sheer exhaustion and frustration, plus the firm stance of the UK and Irish governments, were the essential preconditions to the 1994 ceasefire.

A similar conflict tortured the Lebanon for over a decade after civil war broke out in the mid-1970s. Both local and outside leaders sought peaceful compromise, yet the violence and conflict continued as ethnic and national interests fought for power. A reasonable peace was only restored in 1992 by the intervention of a leader in the form of a businessman-turned-politician, Rafic Hariri, who has applied management solutions to bind up the wounds of an exhausted nation. While his premiership may not prove to be the final chapter in this destructive saga, Hariri displays the leadership traits of Carnegie and other businessmen addressing political conflict. Determined 'to be the one who made a difference' (*Wall Street Journal*, 29 March 1994), Hariri has led by investing his own funds, installing his own staff in government offices, and rebuilding Lebanon's economy. His values and vision are clear; 'I am a simple Lebanese guy who made a fortune in Saudi Arabia ... the more my wealth grew, the more I helped my country. This is in my blood.'

An even longer-lasting struggle has taken place in ancient Palestine dating from before the formation of the Israeli state. A potent mix of fear, anger and religious conflict has failed over the decades to enable a leader either to impose a lasting solution or to negotiate an acceptable compromise. Leaders on both sides of the divide have been unable to bridge the gap between the aspirations and concerns of their own con-stituents and those of the other side. Outside assistance from the US government and United Nations has not provided a leadership solution. Once again, one has the impression that only mutual exhaustion of the virulent opposing forces can create an environment in which leadership can play an effect-ive role. The establishment in Jericho and Gaza of a Palestine government is a major step towards the resolution of this grinding conflict. The leadership historian's interest is thus focused on leaders such as Yasser Arafat to determine whether they have sufficient discipline, empathy and direction to over-come the forces arrayed against them.

In the early 1990s, the violent conflict in the former Yugoslavia captured the world's attention. Here again the latent antagonisms of centuries have boiled over, actually stimulated by local leaders who are leveraging these ethnic and national emotions in some cases for their own political power. At the time of writing this book, no single effective leader like Tito had emerged to provide a mutually accept-able solution to the various warring factions. Instead, a fragile collective leadership imposed by the world's powers appeared to be breaking up under the centrifugal pressure exerted by the major ethnic groups.

Sub-Saharan Africa in the post-colonial era has been a grave-yard of hopes that leadership can overcome deep-seated tribal rivalries and impose the necessary discipline to drive sustained economic growth. Yet South Africa, where apartheid created an extraordinary level of tribal conflict, may offer a successful case-study of leadership from the heads of the country's two largest tribes. The commitment of Nelson Mandela and F.W. de Klerk in 1993 to unite on a common way forward is remarkable in a continent torn by ethnic and political factions. While the ultimate outcome of the country's democratic and multiracial transformation is unclear, the student of leadership can only be fascinated by the presence of two leaders from opposing factions submerging their differences to establish a common political programme.

Of particular fascination to the student of leadership is Nelson Mandela. His unbending direction, sensitivity to the needs of all the ethnic factions in his complex country, and total commitment to a multiracial state fully aligns with the leadership paradigm described in this book. At his trial before imprisonment, he articulated his mission as follows: 'I have fought against white domination, and I have cherished the ideal of a democratic and free society ... it is an ideal for which I am prepared to die' (Rosenbach and Taylor, 1989: 218). After 27 years imprisonment and a bruising battle for the Presidency of South Africa in 1994, the message in his victory speech was basically unchanged: 'I am your servant. I don't come to you as a leader, as one above others. We are a great team... I pledge to use all my strength and ability to live up to your expectations of me... We want every political organization that participates in that government to feel they are part and parcel of a government machine which is happy to accommodate their views' (*Financial Times*, 3 May 1994).

The confrontation of political factions within a given country represents a second category of conflict. Iran, a number of Central and Latin American nations, and now Russia, have suffered from sustained and often violent strife which has posed a major leadership challenge.

From this conflict a number of successful leaders have been able to bind together the warring factions. Often such a resolution has taken years, if not decades, to achieve, and in many cases the struggle continues. Violeta Chamorro in Nicaragua, Ali Akbar Rafsanjani in Iran, Alberto Fujimori in Peru, Augusto Pinochet in Chile, King Hussein in Jordan, as well as constitutional monarchs – King Bhumibol in Thailand and King Juan Carlos in Spain – have all displayed considerable leadership success in this environment. When queried about how Hussein defended Jordanian interests against its stronger neighbours in the 1960s, he responded 'I have always tried my utmost not to let people down in terms of their hopes and expectations… [Jordan] has held its head high and has tried its best' (Stern: 171–80).

A particular phenomenon at the end of the twentieth century has been the break-up of the former Soviet empire, which, while still in the early stages of its evolution, should be a useful test-bed for the effectiveness of leadership in a period of violent change and conflict.

Since Stalin's death, a string of Soviet leaders beginning with Nikita Khruschev has led the process of change in the totalitarian megalith created by Josef Stalin. Mikhail Gorbachev played an essential role in releasing the forces of change in the form of *perestroika* and *glasnost*, but he was incapable of the essential leadership tasks of setting and implementing a viable new direction and appears to have vanished from the political scene. A new leader appeared when another product of the old regime, Boris Yeltsin, stood firm against reactionary forces in defending the White House in 1991 and articulating a new vision of a modern, reformed and open Russia. Yet he too by the time of writing this book had found it difficult to maintain direction, shape opinion in the electorate, and provide the vigorous, determined implementation needed in the chaotic break-up of the former society.

Once again, the way forward at the time of writing is totally unclear, yet in leadership terms the analyst can point once again to the difficulty of any single individual in turbulent times to provide all the requisite skills in meeting the different challenges. Both Yeltsin and Gorbachev have found it is relatively easy to articulate the way forward, yet mobilizing both personal energy and the efforts of a frustrated and angry followership is a much greater challenge.

Another leadership challenge has been to impose sufficient discipline in allocating resources to maximize national economic growth potential and still retain political power in a multiparty democratic environment. This challenge exists in emerging as well as mature markets, but the leadership's task is particularly formidable in democracies where the power of the ballot box, supplemented by outspoken, independent media and articulate opposition parties and factional groups creates a potent challenge to even the most effective leader. Volatile popular opinion, well recorded in incessant polling, has repeatedly thrown putative leaders into the political wilderness when challenged at the ballot box. As pointed out in Chapter 5, cries in these democratic countries for leadership usually constitute in effect an appeal for satisfying the particular interests of these followers. Such cries are particularly strident in countries such as the United States populated by vocal single-issue groups. In this environment it is truly a remarkable individual who can retain a sense of consistent direction, deal sensitively yet firmly with a host of conflicting interests, and personally endure the barrage of criticism he or she receives.

In this context, an interesting case study is that of George Bush in the United States. In the conflict with Iraq over Kuwait, Bush displayed a masterful command of events in carefully orchestrating the support of his domestic constituencies, marshalling the support of allies and the international community, and carrying out a swift military solution thousands of miles from American bases. Yet he left the presidency shortly thereafter, bedevilled by criticism of lacking 'the vision thing', when a combination of economic difficulties and articulate opposition denied him a second term.

Even more interesting for the student of leadership is the case of Margaret Thatcher, whose decade of effective leadership in the United Kingdom in the 1980s recalls that of Charles de Gaulle several decades earlier. Preceded by a series of Prime Ministers unable to rejuvenate the British economy and sense of national purpose, she proceeded with her iron determination to transform the country's culture and economic base. While this inevitably led to resistance and conflict, her ultimate fall from power in the Conservative Party came from a growing awareness that her style, not her vision, would not receive popular support at the next election. Arguably, as in the case of de Gaulle, she had lost touch with her followership and was pursuing policies in Europe and elsewhere which did not find an echo in the electorate despite wide agreement on the value of her economic and political reforms. In the words of one of her former senior ministers, 'the insistence on the undivided sovereignty of her own opinion – dressed up as the nation's sovereignty – was her undoing. The withdrawal of support for her leadership... was a consequence not of malice or weakness but of an increasingly clear perception that her singlemindedness, which once had achieved so much, now threatened to take her party and the nation into the wilderness' (Howe, *Financial Times,* 23 October 1993).

In contrast, Germany since Konrad Adenauer's chancellorship following the Second World War has been directed by a string of effective leaders each committed to building a strong Germany tied to the democratic process and linked closely to its Western allies. While a kaleidoscope of changing coalitions has held power since the 1950s, leaders such as Willy Brandt and Helmut Schmidt have maintained this direction. The most recent Chancellor, Helmut Kohl, continues to absorb criticism from all sides yet maintains direction at the same time as negotiating with a host of constituencies to maintain some consensus on an action programme.

A somewhat different challenge has confronted the leader in an emerging nation – more specifically one which is emerging from totalitarianism or endemic conflict into a sophisticated democratic state with a reasonable consensus on the direction to be taken. Throughout Asia, Latin America and Africa leaders are pursuing the goals of a liberal, open economy and some form of open democratic process which meets the aspirations of its citizens. In each case the successful leader has attracted criticism at home and abroad, yet their achievements in many cases are impressive.

In Asia, President Suharto has displayed all the leadership talents described earlier in this book in building a modern Indonesia. Like Charlemagne, he has been ruthless in marginalizing opposition, yet equally he has supported a meritocratic technocracy which is transforming the Indonesian economy and boosting its standard of living. Although outside critics point to continuing corruption and economic waste, the transformation of Indonesia since the death of Sukarno in the 1960s is largely attributable to the efforts of this single leader.

Another successful, albeit controversial Asian leader is Lee Kuan Yew of Singapore, whose leadership has been instrumental in transforming this small island state from a former British colonial outpost with few natural resources into a wealthy, disciplined and attractive regional financial and industrial centre. As in the case of Indonesia, political opposition has been marginalized, while outside observers criticize the level of discipline imposed on many dimensions of life in the country. Yet the fundamental achievement of Prime Minister Lee is undeniable, and his vision of a modern state has been espoused by many other emerging states. Asked to put his leadership in perspective, he responded 'All I have proved is that if you are determined enough ... you can make a country work with almost all the factors against it, provided everybody knows we are going against the tide and willing to row that way.' (Stern, 1993: 115).

In China, Deng Xiaoping has played a central role both in restoring a political consensus in the way forward and opening up the economy to market forces. A victim himself of the leadership of his predecessor Mao Tse-tung, Deng has been criticized for authoritarian measures such as the Tiananmen Square repression. As in so many other cases, it is too early to make an objective appraisal of the quality of his leadership.

In Europe, the process of emerging from a totalitarian cocoon has produced a number of leaders who have played a central role in driving change. Apart from several democratically elected Prime Ministers, the role of King Juan Carlos in Spain has been critical in the process. When right-wing advocates threatened the democratic process in 1981, the King dramatically descended to the political stage by articulating the national direction before the Cortes and ensuring that the democratic process should continue.

With these examples of contemporary leadership in mind, what can we conclude about the lessons of leadership for our time?

First, it is clear that today's successful leaders reflect the same steadfast direction, sensitivity to the needs of their followership, and determined pursuit of objectives as their predecessors. Lee Kuan Yew, Margaret Thatcher, King Hussein, President Suharto and their peers have distinguished themselves by the same qualities of ruthless determination in pursuit of national goals as such forebears as Bismarck, Ataturk and Peter the Great. By the same token, less successful aspirants in contemporary Russia, sub-Saharan Africa and many Western democracies can be faulted for the lack of these qualities.

However, it is equally clear that even the most successful contemporary leaders are controversial and the subject of fierce opposition. A standard criticism of national leaders like Suharto, Lee, Deng, Fujimori and Thatcher is their authoritarian manner and repression of opposing views. Even thoroughly democratic leaders like Helmut Kohl are viciously attacked from all sides and are subject to plummeting ratings in public opinion polls. In most cases it is premature to draw objective conclusions on the value of their leadership period. Yet such an evaluation, rather than the welter of contemporary slings and arrows which seems inevitably to surround leaders, is the only valid means of distinguishing 'good' from 'bad' leaders.

The welcome extension of democratic traditions which has characterized the late twentieth century has made the difficult task of leadership even more testing. The challenge of the ballot box, coupled with the volatility of an electorate confronted with painful change, has considerably shortened the career of a host of otherwise successful leaders. It is little comfort to such individuals to recall that predecessors such as Abraham Lincoln, Pericles, Charles de Gaulle and Shigeru Yoshida were also tortured by collapsing popular ratings – and often ousted from office as a result of them.

It is clear that the passions released by ethnic, religious and national schism are sufficiently powerful to sweep away for an extended period of time the efforts of even the most talented leaders to bring factions together on a common way forward. The polarization in Northern Ireland and in Palestine thus recalls the emotions of Americans in the 1860s and Frenchmen in the late sixteenth century. In the latter instances years, if not decades, had to pass before even a leader such as Lincoln or Henri IV could shape some form of common ground. And each of these outstanding leaders, as well as Gandhi, who also devoted his life to peaceful compromise, were eventually to lose his life to assassins driven by the hatreds generated by these conflicts.

Not only can would-be leaders struggle unsuccessfully for years to reduce conflict, but they are also quite capable of increasing its intensity. Just as Hitler and Stalin unleashed purges and wars which caused millions of deaths, today factional leaders in the former Soviet Union and Yugoslavia are reopening old schisms as they advance their particular cause.

The fascinating challenge of determining the outcome of the interaction between leadership and external forces remains just that – a challenge. This book did not set out to determine why leaders succeed or fail in given environmental circumstances; our purpose has been simply to establish the common profile of those who succeed. The task of examining, for example, why leadership succeeds in a given period in one country yet not in its neighbouring twin – say, in Morocco and Algeria – is beyond the scope of this book. In 1994 President Bill Clinton seemed to be applying the same leadership approach to key legislation as did his democratic predecessor Woodrow Wilson in 1913, yet with considerably less success. Yet from our research it is clear that the element of chance plays a central role in this complex process. The coincidence of followership needs and a leader's personal direction at a given time and place is not readily predictable. Thus Charles de Gaulle, Winston Churchill and Shigeru Yoshida reappeared on the political scene well after normal retirement age due to a particular confluence of unpredictable external factors.

Finally, the nature of leadership is such that successful candidates may diverge sharply from the wholesome, well-aligned paradigm of today's business literature and the straightfoward role of specific historical leaders such as Washington and Lincoln. The overpowering will and motivation of a leader may express itself in a desire for personal power, arrogance, a weakness for pleasures of the flesh and an unwillingness to brook opposition. The greater the leader, the greater may be these less appetizing qualities. The ultimate challenge to the leadership student is to weigh the various considerations and provide an objective final conclusion on the net value added by such multifaceted individuals.

Bibliography

Adair, John: *Developing Leaders*, Talbot Adair Press, Guildford, Surrey, 1988.
Adair, John: *Great Leaders*, Talbot Adair Press, Guildford, 1980.
Adams, John (ed.): *Transforming Leadership – from Vision to Results*, Miles River Press, Alexandria, Va, 1986.
Auty, Phyllis: *Tito, a Biography*, Longmans, London, 1970.
Bailey, F.G: *Humbuggery and Manipulation: The Art of Leadership*, Cornell University Press, Ithaca, 1988.
Bass, Bernard M.: *Bass & Stogdill's Handbook of Leadership*, 3rd edition, Free Press, New York, 1990.
Bass, Bernard M.: *Leadership and Performance beyond Expectations*, Free Press, New York, 1985.
Bennis, Warren: *On Becoming a Leader*, Addison-Wesley, Reading, Mass., 1989.
Bennis, Warren and Burt Nanus: *Leadership – The Strategies for Taking Charge*, Harper & Row, New York, 1985.
Brabazon, James: *Albert Schweitzer*, Victor Gollancz, London, 1976.
Buckman, Peter: *Lafayette, a Biography*, Paddington Press, London, 1977.
Bullock, Alan: *Hitler and Stalin – Parallel Lives*, HarperCollins, London, 1991.
Burns, James MacGregor: *Leadership*, Harper Torch Books, New York, 1978.
Caraman, Philip: *Ignatius Loyola*, Collins, London, 1990.
Castelot, André: *Henri IV le passioné*, Librairie Academique Perin, Paris, 1986.
Crankshaw, Edward: *Bismarck*, Macmillan, London, 1981.
Crankshaw, Edward: *Maria Theresa*, Longmans Green, London, 1969.
Cronin, Vincent: *Napoleon*, Fontana/Collins, 1971.
De Madariaga, Salvador: *Bolivar*, Hollis & Carter, London, 1952.
Djilas, Milovan: *Tito – the Story from Inside*, Weidenfeld & Nicolson, London, 1981.
Dower, J.W.: *Empire and Aftermath: Yoshida and the Japanese Experience, 1878–1954* Harvard East Asia Monograph No.84: Harvard University Press, Cambridge, Mass., 1988.
Financial Times, 23 October 1993 and 3 May 1994.
Firth, C.H.: *Oliver Cromwell and the Role of the Puritans in England*, G.P. Putnam, 1900.
Fraser, Antonia: *Cromwell – Our Chief of Men*, Panther Books, St. Albans, 1975.
Freeman, Douglas Southall: *Washington*, Macmillan, New York, 1968.
Gardner, John W.: *On Leadership*, Free Press, New York, 1990.
Green, Peter: *Alexander the Great*, Weidenfeld & Nicholson, London, 1970.
Hecksher, August: *Woodrow Wilson, a Biography,* Charles Scribner's Sons, New York, 1991.
Hurst, Quentin: *Henry of Navarre*, Holder and Stoughton, London, 1937.
Jennings, Eugene F.: *An Anatomy of Leadership*, New York Press, 1960.
Kagan, Donald: *Pericles of Athens,* Simon & Schuster, New York, 1991.

Kellerman, Barbara (ed.): *Political Leadership – A Source Book*, University of Pittsburgh Press, Pittsburgh, 1986.

Kellerman, Barbara: *Leadership – Multidisciplinary Perspectives*, Prentice Hall, Englewood Cliffs, NJ, 1984.

Kennedy, John F.: *Profiles in Courage*, Harper & Row, New York, 1956.

Kinross, Lord: *Ataturk – A Biography of Mustafa Kemal*, William Morrow, New York, 1978.

Kotter, John: *The Leadership Factor*, Free Press, New York, 1988.

Kouzes, James and Barry Z. Posner: *The Leadership Challenge*, Jossey-Bass, San Francisco, 1987.

Lacouture, Jean: *De Gaulle – The Ruler: 1945–1970*, Collins Harvill, London, 1991.

Massie, Robert K.: *Peter the Great*, Ballantine Books, New York, 1980.

Payne, Robert: *The Life and Death of Mahatma Gandhi*, Bodley Head, London, 1969.

Pearson, Hesketh: *Henry of Navarre*, William Heinemann, London, 1963.

Ritter, E.A.: *Shaka Zulu*, Longmans Green, London, 1955.

Rosenbach, William and Robert L. Taylor (eds): *Contemporary Issues in Leadership*, 2nd edition, Westview Press, Boulder, Colorado, 1989.

Rubin, Nancy: *Isabella of Castile – The First Renaissance Queen,* St. Martin's Press, New York, 1991.

Sackville-West, Vita: *Saint Joan of Arc*, Doubleday, New York, 1936.

Sandberg, Carl: *Abraham Lincoln – The War Years,* 1861–65, Dell New York, 1954.

Stern, Geoffrey: *Leaders and Leadership*, London School of Economics, 1993.

Syrett, Michael and Clare Hogg (eds): *Frontiers of Leadership*, Blackwell, Oxford, 1992.

Terrill, Ross: *Mao, a Biography*, Harper & Row, New York, 1980.

Todd, John: *Martin Luther*, Burns & Oates, London, 1964.

Wall, Joseph Frazier: *Andrew Carnegie*, Oxford University Press, New York, 1970.

Wall Street Journal, European edition, 29 March 1994.

Warner, Marina: *Joan of Arc: The Image of Female Heroism*, Weidenfeld & Nicolson, London, 1981.

Wills, Garry: *Certain Trumpets*, Simon & Schuster, New York, 1994.

Winston, Richard: *Charlemagne: From the Hammer to the Cross,* Eyre & Spottiswoode, London, 1956.

Woodham-Smith, Cecil: *Florence Nightingale*, Constable, London, 1950.

Index